Praise for *Not from Around Here*

This book fills me with hope that Christians can love and learn from each other across the differences that make us sometimes feel like enemies. Brandon O'Brien's personal narrative models the empathy and humility needed by all—rural, suburban, and urban. I echo his prayers that we'll find our shared identity in Christ and not primarily in our zip code.

COLLIN HANSEN
Editorial director of The Gospel Coalition and author of *Blind Spots: Becoming a Courageous, Compassionate, and Commissioned Church*

It is hard to escape the constant inundation of noise that reminds us of our distances from each other, which made *Not from Around Here* a truly delightful read. This is an enjoyable and convicting book that stirred a longing for more exploration around what is common in the midst of our diverse histories and backgrounds.

DENNAE PIERRE
Executive Director of the Surge Network, a group of 60 churches working together to be a witness for Jesus and plant more churches in the Phoenix metro area

To read *Not from Around Here* is to be reminded of the importance of good stories, which traffic in the concrete rather than the abstract. Having lived most of the diverse geographical places O'Brien has lived, I might not have thought I needed these stories. Turns out, I did. I needed O'Brien's clarion call to remember that my primary identity is not now as a resident of North America's fourth-largest city. I'm a Christian before an urbanite, and my brothers and sisters in hollers and small-towns and suburban tract neighborhoods have much to teach me. This book was a pleasure to read and will be an honor to recommend.

JEN POLLOCK MICHEL
Author of *Keeping Place* and *Surprised by Paradox*

How do you cultivate a theology of place when the place you practice theology keeps changing? It's a question I ask often because I have spent my adult life living in almost a dozen different states. When asked, I am *never* from around here. Brandon O'Brien has captured this sense of alien homelessness in an acute way as he moves his readers through his transient life in the country, the suburbs, a small city, and an urban place. He gives his readers some handrails to hold onto in an ever-changing terrain, and reminds us where our true home really is.

LORE FERGUSON WILBERT
Author of *Handle with Care*

In a divided America, we need empathetic storytellers who can show us (rather than simply tell) how the places we live form our loves. *Not from Around Here* travels from rural America, to the suburbs, and lands in New York City to gently expose the myth we believe: that there is a single story about place. But the story of the gospel is bigger than that. O'Brien offers hope that as Christians embrace our primary identity as followers of Christ, we can begin to heal our divisions. Engaging, funny, insightful, and warm, *Not from Around Here* shows us how to get home.

ASHLEY HALES
Author of *Finding Holy in the Suburbs: Living Faithfully in the Land of Too Much*

NOT FROM AROUND HERE

WHAT UNITES US, WHAT DIVIDES US, AND HOW WE CAN MOVE FORWARD

BRANDON J. O'BRIEN

Moody Publishers

CHICAGO

Names and details of some stories have been changed to protect the privacy of individuals.

Chapter 8 includes an excerpt from the author's blog post "Gifts from Worshipping in a Multiethnic Urban Church," Redeemer City to City, Medium.com, April 23, 2018.

Unless otherwise indicated, Scripture quotations are from the ESV® Bible (The Holy Bible, English Standard Version®), copyright © 2001 by Crossway Bibles, a publishing ministry of Good News Publishers. Used by permission. All rights reserved.

Scripture quotations marked NASB are from the New American Standard Bible®, Copyright © 1960, 1962, 1963, 1968, 1971, 1972, 1973, 1975, 1977, 1995 by The Lockman Foundation. Used by permission.

Scripture quotations marked (NLT) are taken from the Holy Bible, New Living Translation, copyright © 1996, 2004, 2015 by Tyndale House Foundation. Used by permission of Tyndale House Publishers, Inc., Carol Stream, Illinois 60188. All rights reserved.

Scripture quotations marked (NIV) are taken from the Holy Bible, New International Version®, NIV®. Copyright © 1973, 1978, 1984, 2011 by Biblica, Inc.™ Used by permission of Zondervan. All rights reserved worldwide. www.zondervan.com. The "NIV" and "New International Version" are trademarks registered in the United States Patent and Trademark Office by Biblica, Inc.™

Scripture quotations marked KJV are taken from the King James Version.

All emphasis in Scripture has been added.

Edited by Amanda Cleary Eastep and Mackenzie Conway
Interior design: Ragont Design
Cover design: Dean Renninger
Cover photo of plowing fields copyright © 2018 by tunart / iStock (950785056).
Cover photo of city intersection copyright © 2019 by Chris Clor / Getty Images (605763565).
Cover photo of construction site copyright © 2019 by Jung Getty / Getty Images (1026631574). All rights reserved for all photos above.

Library of Congress Cataloging-in-Publication Data

Names: O'Brien, Brandon J., author.
Title: Not from around here : what unites us, what divides us, and how we can move forward / Brandon J. O'Brien.
Description: Chicago : Moody Publishers, [2019] | Includes bibliographical references. |
Identifiers: LCCN 2019017472 (print) | LCCN 2019020749 (ebook) | ISBN 9780802496560 | ISBN 9780802416964
Subjects: LCSH: O'Brien, Brandon J. | United States--Social life and customs--1971---Anecdotes. | Christian life--United States.
Classification: LCC E169.Z83 (ebook) | LCC E169.Z83 O33 2019 (print) | DDC 973.924--dc23
LC record available at https://lccn.loc.gov/2019017472

All websites and phone numbers listed herein are accurate at the time of publication but may change in the future or cease to exist. The listing of website references and resources does not imply publisher endorsement of the site's entire contents. Groups and organizations are listed for informational purposes, and listing does not imply publisher endorsement of their activities.

We hope you enjoy this book from Moody Publishers. Our goal is to provide high-quality, thought-provoking books and products that connect truth to your real needs and challenges. For more information on other books and products written and produced from a biblical perspective, go to www.moodypublishers.com or write to:

Moody Publishers
820 N. LaSalle Boulevard
Chicago, IL 60610

1 3 5 7 9 10 8 6 4 2

Printed in the United States of America

For Grandmother and Granddaddy
You will always be true home for me.

Contents

*"Life can only be understood backwards,
but it must be lived forwards."*

Søren Kierkegaard

This Is How It Is with Us: An Introduction

"Remember when we lived in America?"

This is how my son would introduce memories about our life in Arkansas during the first year we lived in New York City.

Remember when we lived in America, and we could go fishing any time we wanted?

Remember when we lived in America, and we rode in a car every day?

Remember when we lived in America, and we never saw anyone pee on the sidewalk?

"We still live in America," I told him again and again. "New York is *in* America."

He was not easily convinced.

In fairness to my perceptive youngster, he was onto something. My wife, Amy, and I sold most of our things, including two cars and a house, and moved our two kids from a 1,500-square-foot home on a quarter-acre lot to a small apartment in Uptown Manhattan. We exchanged a privacy fence for public transportation. We exchanged playing with a few neighbors in the cul-de-sac for playing with several dozen strangers on a playground.

We didn't move the kids to a different country. We *did* move them to a different America.

What our children don't know is that a lot of people questioned our move. Folks said, "I just can't *imagine* living there." In part, they meant they couldn't imagine living in a small apartment and being surrounded by concrete and steel. They also meant they couldn't imagine living among the kinds of people who live in cities, *city* people, with their "different" values.

Our kids don't realize—though someday they will—that we don't just live in a different America now. We live in a divided America.

Here's a list—not exhaustive—of the things that divide us Americans, including Americans who are also Christians.

- We are divided by how we make money, how much money we make, and how we spend the money we have.[1]
- We are divided by race and ethnicity; that is, we experience feelings of estrangement from one another along racial and ethnic lines, *and* peoples' experience of life in these United States varies based on their race or ethnicity.[2]
- We are divided by politics, as our public discourse is increasingly polarized between Left and Right, Blue and Red, liberal and conservative, with very little interest in cooperating across the aisle.[3]
- We are divided by where we get our news, and therefore our perception of the major issues of our generation and their possible solutions.[4]
- We are divided by entertainment—what movies we watch, what shows we stream, what music we listen to.[5]

It's a lot. And this isn't all of it. It is, however, enough to illustrate the point that America is divided along a lot of lines and over a lot of issues. Because these conversations are complicated and difficult, all this complexity is often simplified into one big division, a division that summarizes them all: the urban/rural divide.

Turn on a cable news network (it doesn't matter which one) and before long you will have the impression that America is composed of two regions: urban and rural. These two regions are pitched in a life-and-death battle over essential values. They have competing versions of the American dream, fundamentally opposite visions of the good life. They disagree about sexuality, gender and race relations, immigration—you name it. To an unprecedented degree, "we're in a political moment where cultural divides overlap with political divides, which overlap with geography."[6] All manner of cultural and political animus has been gathered up and handed out in two lumps to rural and urban America.

Of course this is an oversimplification. These two categories—urban and rural—exclude the place most Americans live: the suburbs. The categorization of "two Americas" flattens distinctions such as between small towns and "the country." It implies that everyone in every city shares the same values. One of the goals of this book is to frustrate these tidy categories and help us appreciate the complexity and diversity of the different places we all call home.

In any case, there is plenty of data to confirm that Americans feel divided from one another based on their geography.

According to Pew Research Center, 65 percent of urban dwellers and 70 percent of rural dwellers feel that "most people who live in different types of communities don't understand the problems they face." Nearly equal percentages of urban and rural people say "people who don't live in their type of community have a negative view of those who do."[7]

Politicians have weaponized these feelings. The presidential election of 2016 was cast as a battle, by all involved, between two Americas: the America of the heartland stands for traditional American values and faith and neighborliness and the America of the coasts stands for progressive (probably European) values and secularism and greed.

Christians in America carry all this cultural baggage with them into the church.[8] In the last year I've read three books about ministry and the Christian life. Each is set in a different region of the country. All of them claim their region is neglected by the broader Christian community.

A number of books encourage Christians to think about American cities as mission fields because Christians are underrepresented in cities. Christians make up a higher percentage of the general population in suburbs, small towns, and rural areas than in cities. Cities are growing, and there aren't enough churches to reach the population with the gospel of Jesus. Our cities are neglected, they say.

Meanwhile a number of books and articles from advocates for rural ministry lament that American Christians have turned their entire attention to cities, lured by the glamour of urban life, and have abandoned the heartland. "Rural America is rapidly becoming a spiritual wasteland, where churches are being closed because they are overlooked and cast aside by the larger church community as a place deemed too insignificant or unworthy of our attention."[9] The rural areas are neglected.

A recent book about life in the suburbs claimed that all attention is now paid to urban and rural places. "More than 50 percent of Americans live in suburbs, and many of them desire to live a Christian life. Yet often the suburbs are ignored ... denigrated and demeaned ... or seen as a cop-out to a faithful Christian life."[10] The suburbs are neglected.

It's an interesting situation when Christians everywhere feel neglected by all the Christians everywhere else.

My experience in both rural and urban settings is that a person's Christian faith has very little influence on how they view people from another region of the country

It's an interesting situation when Christians everywhere feel neglected by all the Christians everywhere else.

or another type of community. Rural Christians are likely to assume that a person from a city has urban values—values that differ from their own—rather than assume that they may share Christian values, regardless of their geography. When I shared about this book project with family and friends early on, someone I respect summarized the urban/rural divide this way: "It comes down to the Bible and the Constitution. We [i.e., country people] respect those documents and they [i.e., city people] don't." Urban Christians have opposing and equally strong opinions. One friend expressed his view on

Even within the church, we may view people who live in different kinds of places first as our enemies rather than as brothers and sisters in Christ.

social media this way: "Rural and suburban Evangelical cult members are ruining this country and the church." Even within the church, we may view people who live in different kinds of places first as our enemies rather than as brothers and sisters in Christ.

"This Is How It Is with Us"

This is heavy stuff, I know. If you are a Christian, you might be wondering what light the Bible can shed on these issues. The answer depends on how you understand the problem. On the one hand, there is evidence in the New Testament that God's chosen people, the Jews, judged one another based on where they were from. For example, after Jesus called Philip to be His disciple, Philip was so excited he wanted to share the news with his friend Nathanael. Philip told Nathanael, "We have found him of whom Moses in the Law and also the prophets wrote, Jesus of Nazareth, the son of Joseph" (John 1:45).

Nathanael's response reveals how he felt about backwater Nazareth: "Can anything good come out of Nazareth?" (John 1:46).

Beyond passages like this, the Bible doesn't have a lot to say about rural, suburban, and urban places. It does, however, have a lot to say about how people who find their identity in Christ ought to relate to each other, even if they are radically divided by viewpoints about money, politics, race, and morality. My favorite example comes from Mark 2, when Jesus calls an unsavory fella as one of His initial disciples.

In Mark 1, Jesus calls four men to follow Him. They are two sets of brothers: Peter and Andrew (1:16–18) and James and John (1:19–20). Jesus meets them while He is walking along the Sea of Galilee because the four men are all fishermen.

Jesus is once again walking "beside the sea" when He calls another disciple. This man is a Jew like the four fishermen, but that's where the similarities end. This disciple, Levi, is a tax collector. Men in his profession were considered traitors because they were employed by the Roman Empire, the political superpower that oppressed the Jews. Tax collectors made their living by charging their countrymen more taxes than they legally owed and pocketing the difference. That means Levi and the other disciples were different economically: they were "blue collar" workers, and he was a "white collar" worker, wealthier than they were. They were different politically: they resisted the empire, and he was in cahoots with the power that oppressed them. They were different religiously: they had a more conservative understanding of God's law and he, by virtue of his profession, rejected portions of God's law. They were economically, politically, and morally different.

The most remarkable thing about this story, though, is *where* Levi was a tax collector. He collected taxes *by the sea* (Mark 2:13). This means most likely that Levi's job was to collect taxes from fishermen—fishermen like Peter and Andrew and James and John. It's safe to assume, although the Bible doesn't specify, that these men knew Levi and despised him—not just theoretically but *personally*—because he had been fleecing them for years.

Which makes it all the more remarkable when Jesus walks by and says, "Follow me," that Levi does just that. "He rose and followed him" (Mark 2:14).

In the next sentence, Jesus and His disciples are attending a party at Levi's house. The guest list is made up of "tax collectors and sinners" (Mark 2:15). When the Jewish religious leaders question what Jesus and His followers are doing associating with people like this—a question Jesus' other disciples are no doubt asking too—Jesus gives this famous answer: "Those who are well have no need of a physician, but those who are sick. I came not to call the righteous, but sinners" (Mark 2:17).

Jesus' response to the religious leaders is also a message to His disciples. It's as if Jesus is saying to them, *This is how it is with us. Wherever you're from and however you make your living and no matter your political alliances, you have a new source of identity and mission: Me.*

For three years these men (and seven others) followed Jesus from town to town listening and watching as He proclaimed the gospel. There is no record of the conversations they had as they walked, but I have to believe Peter grilled Levi about his past as a tax collector. I have to believe that Levi held onto some of his viewpoints, even as they all gradually understood the kingdom of God Jesus came to inaugurate. I have to believe James and John expected Levi to foot the bill now and then when they bought provisions for their journeys—after all, he could *afford* it. I have to believe there were arguments and disagreements. But they struggled through them together. Because Jesus invites us to engage with each other differently than the world does. This is how it is with us.

A Dog in the Fight

This conversation is deeply personal for me. I grew up in small-town Arkansas and passed most of the weekends, holidays, and summer vacations of my childhood in rural Arkansas and Louisiana. After college, my wife and I lived in the Chicago suburbs for nearly a decade before moving, briefly, back to Arkansas. Now we live in Manhattan. While my wife grew up in Singapore, and is therefore a "city girl" by upbringing, New York City was an entirely unfamiliar place for both of us and our two young children. Like everyone, I have my preferences. But I have sincerely enjoyed living in all of these different places and, more to the point, we have found deep friendship in and experienced profound hospitality from people from rural, small-town, suburban, and urban America . . . people who are ethnically different from us, who have different political opinions, and who experience different economic realities. I've defended all these people when Christians in other places say disparaging things about them.

Which is all to say, I'm invested. Or, to use a good country idiom, I have "a dog in this fight."

Not only have I lived in each of these regions, I've also been involved in ministry in each. I pastored a small church in rural Arkansas during and after college. I served as a deacon at our suburban church in Illinois and worked in Christian publishing for a magazine dedicated to equipping pastors for ministry. I earned degrees in Christian history with a plan to teach in a Christian college or seminary, which is what led me back to Arkansas, where I helped launch a satellite campus for my alma mater. Our program had the unique emphasis of preparing students for local church ministry while they earned a liberal arts degree. In 2017 my family moved to Manhattan, where I am the Director of Content Development and Distribution for Redeemer City to City, an organization that provides specialized training and support for church planters who are starting new churches in cities around the world. My opinions and reflections in these pages are shaped both by my own experience as well as by hours of conversation with pastors in contexts as dissimilar as the rural Pacific Northwest and the urban Northeast and everywhere in between.

I've written several books in the last decade, too, about a range of topics from ministry to biblical interpretation to Christian history.[11] The approach of this book is informed by all this background. My background informs the questions I ask and where I look for answers. For example, one consistent theme in all these projects is the ways our cultural context influences how we imagine and live the Christian life.

In the end, though, I did not write this book as an expert in sociology or politics or economics—although I did consult experts in these fields as I wrote. (Follow the endnotes, if you're interested.) I've done my best to do my homework, but mostly I'm writing as a Christian for whom the sound-bite explanations about why we are divided and what to do about it just aren't satisfying. We live in a historic moment in which Christians across America are divided by regional values rather than being united by Christian values; they feel neglected, wherever they live, when the realities of others elsewhere receive attention. We are basing our most important decisions on beliefs about others that aren't founded in facts but

We live in a historic moment in which Christians across America are divided by regional values rather than being united by Christian values.

in spin and hearsay. We need an exercise in empathy. We need to find common cause. And we need to emphasize our shared identity in Christ over our divided identity as citizens of different parts of the country.

I'm writing from the firm conviction that no one else will do it. It has to be the church.

In the chapters that follow, I hope to start a conversation. These chapters include data about trends and other information intended to provide a bit of perspective on our national landscape. But mostly these chapters include stories. The best way to get to know a place is to live there. The next best is to immerse yourself in stories about that place. So I offer here stories about the places I've lived in hopes that they will help you understand and appreciate them better. I also suggest ways to find common cause and move forward together.

Let's begin.

1

A Nice Place to Belong To

"A man belongs to this world before
he begins to ask if it is nice to belong to it."

—G. K. Chesterton, *Orthodoxy*[1]

As soon as the temperatures begin to rise and the daylight hours lengthen in the early summer, Dad often picks me up from school and drives me straight to the creek to fish until dark.

It is a short drive north on Highway 71 to the next town and Little Sugar Creek, which winds through the Bella Vista Country Club golf course. Dad drives with the windows down and the radio up. The songs at the top of the charts circa 1990 give me glimpses of life in worlds far away. Elton John sings about a club at the end of the street. Don Henley describes how, "In a New York Minute," everything can change. Cher sings about turning back time. I, for one, am quite fine with the time I'm in.

Dad parks the truck along the highway near our favorite

fishing hole and hides the keys in the rear bumper. We walk back upstream as far as we want before scrambling down the bank into the water to fish. Then we wade and fish our way downstream in the direction of the truck.

Little Sugar Creek is typical of Northwest Arkansas waterways. It is narrow, in many places just a few feet across and maybe a dozen yards across at the widest. The banks are covered in rocks the size of grapefruits and here and there jut up in high rocky bluffs. The water is clear as glass and home to hungry smallmouth. The smallmouth are why we are here.

In addition to fishing, I have two jobs.

One is catching crawfish to use as bait—small ones about the length of a pinky finger. There's an art to catching crawfish in a creek, if you want to know the truth. They are small and quick and camouflaged to match the creek bed, and they live under stones. To give yourself the best chance of success, you have to stand with your feet downstream of the rock you plan to look under, so that the moving water will carry the sand and dirt you stir up downstream and out of your way. Then you have to move the stone slowly, so the crawfish doesn't startle and bolt. Move the stone. Let the sand settle. Half the time, there's no crawfish under there anyway and you have to start over elsewhere. If there is one there, you approach from behind, slowly, and pin it between forefinger and thumb. Its little pinchers will shoot up in protest or despair, but you've got it.

This job is perfect for the nimble fingers of a child. I am good at it.

My other job is collecting golf balls from the creek bed

that I later clean—a quick bleach bath and a little scrubbing get rid of the algae—and sell to Dad's coworkers, some for a quarter each and some for fifty cents. By the end of an evening—a good evening—we might be walking back to the truck with a stringer full of smallmouth and pockets bulging with golf balls.

Wading the Little Sugar always feels mildly subversive. We are not allowed to use the golf course; it is a perk reserved for those who own property in the community. We rent. But the Property Owners Association doesn't own the water. We can wend through the course via the creek bed, a quiet and harmless infiltration into a world from which I sometimes feel excluded. Down here we are hiding in plain sight. The gurgle of the creek obscures any noise from the highway. The high banks shorten our horizons. We are not far from home, but we are long gone.

The game of golf, going on above and around us, is an occasional reminder that we are at least adjacent to civilization. Golf holds no appeal to me. Now and then a golfer shanks a ball into the creek and asks us to find it for him.

"What are you guys doing down there?" they ask. "Fishing?"

They say "you guys" instead of "y'all" because they're not from around here. Many of the golfers are retired and have moved to Bella Vista from far off places like Minnesota, Illinois, and Michigan. They have funny accents and belong to foreign religions like Lutheranism.

"Yessir," we say. "Fishing."

"I wish I was doing *that* and you were playing my round of golf."

I can sell an egg carton of secondhand golf balls for up to $6 to guys like these, and the upside of making a little money from Yankee transplants or corporate big shots isn't lost on me.

This is how the values of a place are passed from one generation to the next. They are caught in creeks or on city sidewalks or suburban cul-de-sacs. They are transmitted by experience. There wasn't a catechism class or values seminar for young people in my hometown. There were just days like these, filled mostly with mundane things that shaped my perceptions of the good life and what's important and how to attain and secure the things in life that matter. All of us pick these things up as children without testing them or examining them. No one lays out the options and asks us to choose. (That's what college is for.) We just go to the creek with the windows down on a warm day in early summer and the moment implants things in your soul. Later your parents and neighbors and people you love say things that reinforce those lessons you pick up in the air without thinking. And on it goes.

G. K. Chesterton wrote, "A man belongs to this world before he begins to ask if it is nice to belong to it."[2] He was talking about the cosmos, I suspect, but he could as easily have been talking about the places we grow up. I belonged to rural and small-town Arkansas before I had reason or opportunity to ask if it was nice to belong to it. It's the same for urbanites, too. New Yorkers are brought up believing New York is a nice place to belong to. Same goes for suburbanites, surely.

Different people begin questioning the niceness of their

place of origin at different ages and for different reasons. Good friends of mine were eager to leave our small town before I was. They had considered it not nice before I had given it any thought. Some people never doubt the niceness of their place. In any case, our place makes its mark on us before we are able to question it. We all internalize habits of mind, preferences, and values before we're even conscious that we're from someplace. Once we do, we are shaped forever by either accepting or rejecting the values we grew up with.

This may be obvious, but it's worth coming out and saying. Because most of the time when news outlets and historians and sociologists research and report on the differences between values in urban and rural places, they don't talk about childhood experiences. They don't talk about how the winding, two-lane highway makes you drive slower and how the squish of creek water between your toes shapes your sense of normal and good and right. Instead they compare statistics about crime and education, cross-reference voting patterns and average IQs. They assess media coverage of important events in different regions and analyze Nielsen ratings and median incomes. The most sympathetic treatments at least talk to real people in real places. But even then, they are usually trying to ferret out what a place's values *are*. Rarely do they ask where those values come from or how those values come to take such deep root in the hearts of a local population. An out-of-town researcher would do well to turn off the voice recorder and stand knee-deep in Little Sugar Creek for an afternoon before asking the locals how they feel about climate change and government overreach.

I have my granddaddy's receding hairline and my grand-pa's ruddy complexion. I walk with my dad's gait. And when I sing in a group, I instinctively sing the alto part because that's how my grandmother taught me to harmonize during long drives in the car, before I knew enough to resist. Blame nature or nurture. Either way, I came by all those things honestly. More to the point, none of these things would come out in an interview. If you were to sit me down and ask me about my political affiliation and how I feel about the burning issues of the day, no question I know of would get me thinking about hairlines and singing harmony on road trips. No question would get me thinking about Little Sugar Creek. But those are the kinds of things that make the deepest impression.

The point is, we're all from some*place*, and that someplace shapes us before we are aware of it. Place is not genetic in the same way as our complexion or hairline, but it might as well be. Because before we can resist it, our someplace makes its impression. It gets down in our bones and shapes how we move about in the world. Whether you spend the rest of your life committed to living in and defending your place of origin or trying to leave it behind, that place serves forever as the point of reference, the point of departure. It is the thing you are forever trying to reclaim or forever trying to escape.

The gentlemen driving golf balls over our heads while we fished the Little Sugar Creek, these transplants from north-ern cities like Chicago or Minneapolis or Omaha, moved to Bella Vista for the mild winters and cheap real estate. I didn't know any of that. All I knew was that after spending a whole life somewhere else, they left those northern cities and chose *this* place to retire and die in. I might have been too young to ask the question, but it seemed like these people had asked it and answered it: this really was a nice place to belong to.

A Better Place to Belong to Than Others

Which brings up the other side of this issue. At the same time that we are getting to know our home place deeply and intimately by experience, we are forming opinions about other places in a very different way. While I was learning that my place was a nice place to belong to, I was learning that other places—especially northern cities—were dreadful. The old men who golfed above our heads on Little Sugar Creek taught me that. If *our* place wasn't better than wherever they came from, then why did they come all this way to retire? Songs on the radio reinforced the feeling that the coasts were morally degenerate places. Images on the news reinforced the danger inherent in other places. We watched Rodney King beaten by police in Los Angeles from our living room in an all-white world. A few years later I stood in my baseball uniform, late for a game, while police and news crews pursued O. J. Simpson down a Los Angeles freeway. All of this subtly reinforced a clear message that the place I lived in was better than those places: safer, kinder, more Christian.

By the time I was a teenager, I had formed strong opinions about parts of the country I had never visited and people whom I had never met. I knew those people and those places only by hearsay through media of various sorts.

If the statistics can be trusted, this is how most Americans get their opinions about the *rest* of America. Our main sources of strong opinions about other places are media, whether news outlets, popular music, or television and film. We don't know the places we dislike from up close. We only know them from a distorting distance. If the statistics can be trusted, the average American has visited only ten of our fifty states. That means 80 percent of the country is foreign to most of us. Ten percent of Americans have never traveled outside of the state they live in.[3] And while movies portray families from all over the country making long drives or flights to be home for the holidays, half of Americans live within eighteen miles of their mother. Only 20 percent of us live further than two hours' drive away from our parents.[4] Taken together, this data suggests that Americans actually have very little experience with or exposure to parts of the country and communities unlike the ones they live in.

For most Americans, then, if you want to understand and appreciate the way other people live, it's going to take a concerted effort to do so. It may be as difficult as changing the way you walk or singing the melody when you've been singing harmony all your life. It's worth establishing that point from the beginning. The work this book will ask you to do won't be easy.

The Twenty Percent

Of course there is that twenty percent of folks who live more than two hours from mom, who have experienced a bit more of the world. Some of them leave because they have to. Some leave because they want to. Some people reject the place that first formed them and spend the rest of their life trying to leave it behind.

Others of us moved for different reasons. I followed a calling. There were never any hard feelings. I never rejected my home place. But I left it. In leaving it, I've received the rare gift of living in a range of places: the small-town and rural South; the suburban Midwest; the urban East Coast. Living different places forced me to question and assess the narratives we have received about other places—and our own places—in the media and our own folklore. For me, this ongoing process has unfolded as a series of confrontations.

The first confrontation came right on the eve of adulthood.

My fiancée (now wife) and I were spending the holiday with my dad and stepmom and the extended O'Brien clan at Dad's relatively new cabin on the banks of the White River in north central Arkansas. The location is about as remote as you can imagine—two miles down a dirt road from the nearest town, which has a population of sixty people. By day, Dad's back porch offers a stunning view of the White River winding through sheer Ozark Mountain bluffs. At night, being miles from the nearest street lamp, Dad's front porch gives access to a stunning view of our galaxy. Flip off the porch light and stand in awe of the dazzling curtain of stars.

That's what I did. Amy and I arrived at the house late. Before we went inside, I stopped her on the porch and said, "You've got to see this." I reached inside and turned off the porch light. Had we not been holding hands, we wouldn't have been able to find each other standing nearby. The darkness was profound.

Amy grew up in an Asian city as an American expatriate. Her childhood was about as urban and first-world as they come. I was eager to introduce her to the charms of country living.

"OK, that's enough," she said. "Turn the lights on."

I was surprised. "But isn't this view spectacular? Isn't it *romantic*?"

"Sure. It's also creeping me out. Let's go inside."

"Wait just a second. What's creepy about it? It's just you and me and this unbelievable light show."

"Right," she said. "Just *you* and *me*. In the middle of nowhere. With no witnesses. What if something terrible happens to us out here? No one would know. There's a reason all the horror movies happen in places like this."

"You mean you'd feel safer if there were more people around—more lights and noise and all that—even if the people were strangers?"

"Absolutely."

"Well, if something terrible happens to you out here, maybe no one will know," I said. "I'll give you that. But if something terrible happens to you in a city, no one will *care*. I'd rather take my chances in the country."

"Feel free. I'm going inside."

This was the first time in our relationship it occurred to me we might not see eye to eye on every issue.

We went inside where everyone was already asleep. She went to bed in the downstairs guest room. I went upstairs and slept on the loft overlooking the living room, troubled by my fiancée's failure to recognize the commonsensical superiority of rural life.

The next morning, in the gray light of dawn, I was awakened from sleep when I heard my dad say something I had only heard him say when we were hunting doves or ducks or some other sort of bird:

"They're coming in heavy now." He said it from the living room below me. Before I could ask myself why he would say something like that from the living room—*were birds landing on the furniture?*—I got an answer. There was a wall-shaking boom. Someone had fired a gun. In the house.

I sat upright to yell downstairs, "What's going—" Before I could ask the question, another round went off. Below I saw my dad sitting cross-legged on the floor just inside the back door. The door was ajar, just wide enough to accommodate the barrel of a hunting rifle, which Dad still shouldered. He and the stock of the gun were inside; the business end of the barrel was outside.

"Dad! What in the world are you doing?" It was the only reasonable question to ask.

He looked up at me and gave what he considered the only reasonable response: "Well, if I open the door any wider, they fly away."

"Uh huh."

"This way I can just shoot from inside, and they don't fly away."

"Dad. It's 6 a.m."

He looked around him. "It looks like everyone's up."

He was right. A couple rounds of gunfire will have that effect. My grandparents were on the stairs, disheveled, in their nightclothes. Their faces said, *It's early, but this isn't the most surprising thing that could have happened in this place at this hour.* My fiancée (who, it should be noted, was not yet legally bound to this clan) was at the bottom of the stairs in her pajamas, looking at my dad who had just fired a gun in the house at six in the morning on Thanksgiving. When I looked at her looking at us, it was like I saw my family for the first time. The scales fell from my eyes. How did I not see it before now?

This is not normal behavior.

Except that for the previous twenty-something years of my life, it had been. It took me seeing my people and my place through someone else's eyes to make the truth plain. And there was no unseeing the truth once it was revealed.

No one who knows us would characterize my family as "rednecks." Most of my family members are accomplished white-collar professionals of various sorts. We just hunted and fished and ate wild game. We worked hard and earned money so we could vacation in the middle of nowhere. Other branches of my family, my mom's side, had different hobbies but chose a remote lifestyle, too, on the banks of a bayou in Louisiana. These experiences made us different and they shaped me considerably. And now, for the first time in my life, I was seeing what we must look like to outsiders.

Just a few weeks later, Amy and I married and moved to the Chicago suburbs, where I had the chance to become familiar with the kinds of people who moved to my hometown to retire. Relationships there changed the way I viewed

Northern transplants and the cities and suburbs they moved from. Those relationships also changed the way I viewed the small town I grew up in and the ways of living I considered normal and right. Through these experiences I realized that understanding other people better can result in your understanding yourself better. That's why we need each other—to help us see what we can't see alone.

But now I'm getting ahead of myself. There's more about all that to come.

Before we go much further, we'll do our best to agree on the terms of the conversation that follows. Join me in the next chapter.

2

What We Mean When We Talk About "Urban" and "Rural" America

"You keep using that word. I do not think it means what you think it means."

—Inigo Montoya, *The Princess Bride*

Now is as good a time as any to define our terms.

We are working under the assumption that urban and rural America, including the church, is divided by irreconcilable differences in values. We had better make sure we know what we mean when we say "urban" and "rural."

This sounds like the easiest part of the process.

I assure you it is not.

Ask five different people what the words mean, and you'll get five different answers. When I asked my grandmother how she would define "urban," she said, "When I was a kid, an 'urban' experience was riding my uncle's cotton wagon up the road to the gin in Sibley." Sibley, Louisiana, had a population of around

400 in 1940. It had a cotton gin, a butcher, and a grocer. By comparison to my grandmother's homestead, it was the big city.

To take a more contemporary example, one popular blogger published a book in 2018 in which she chronicled her family's move from "the farmhouse we loved and the small-town life where we fit right in" to become an "urban family" in a nearby city.[1] The city to which she moved has a population of 33,000. Any New Yorker I know would laugh at the thought of applying the label "urban" to a town that size. The *neighborhood* in which I live in Upper Manhattan has a population of nearly 300,000 in just a few square miles.

If you are dealing with the general public, then, the answer to the question, "What do we mean by 'urban' and 'rural'?" is, "It depends who you ask."

The situation is not vastly improved when you ask the experts. The United States government defines "rural" at least fifteen different ways. The Census Bureau, for example, defines "rural" as "any place outside a town, city, or 'urban cluster' with more than 2,500 residents." Sometimes the same agency defines rural differently for different purposes. When it comes to issuing loans and grants for "community facilities," for example, the Department of Agriculture defines rural as "any place with 20,000 or fewer inhabitants." But when determining areas to serve with water and waste-disposal systems, rural means any place with 10,000 or fewer inhabitants.[2]

To summarize, according to the American federal government, a rural area may be a place with 20,000 inhabitants, 10,000 inhabitants, or fewer than 2,500 inhabitants.

Confused? Me too.

Not Just One or the Other

Part of the challenge in defining terms is that so much of the conversation in America uses only these two terms—urban and rural—to describe *all* of the nation's geography. This happens in part because since 1870, the designations "urban" and "rural" are the US Census Bureau's only two geographic categories. Since the early twentieth century, "urban" has meant a census tract containing at least 2,500 people and "rural" is anything that isn't urban. The Census Bureau's definitions have become more sophisticated over time. But a problem remains. Because two, and only two, categories are in operation, the terms flatten out the complexity of the American landscape. "According to the Census Bureau, a place is 'urban' if it's a big, modest or even very small collection of people living near each other. That includes Houston, with its 4.9 million people, and Bellevue, Iowa, with its 2,543."[3] In other words, a place can be "urban" without being what anyone would consider a "city."

In fact, the term "urban," the way it is used in media and political discourse and even by the Census Bureau, *includes* another enormously important category: suburbs. "Official government data obscures how suburban America really is."[4] A little more than half of the nation's population lives in a suburban area—neither rural nor city.[5] And the suburbs are growing at a faster rate than the cities.[6] But defining "suburb" is not as simple as it sounds.

Suburbs are historically residential areas connected to an urban center. But beyond the lexical definition, there is also a *quality* or *feel* that people often associate with suburbs: rows of cookie-cutter houses, big-box stores, chain restaurants. If you think of suburbs this way, less about *where they are* in relation to a city and more about what they are *like*, then many small towns and small cities across America have a suburban feel, even if they lack proximity to an urban place. I've heard long-time New Yorkers complain about the suburbanization of the Upper West Side in the years that we've lived in Manhattan.

This gets us to another way to clarify what we're talking about. For many people, the terms "rural," "urban," and "suburban" carry connotations beyond geography. For some, rural places have predominantly white and often poor populations, while suburbs are predominantly white and upper middle class. For others, "urban" conjures images of poor minorities, especially African Americans. That is, of course, unless we're talking about "urban elites," which are typically perceived to be rich, liberal white folks. Again, among the experts, connotations become a sort of shorthand for various purposes. A Republican strategist noted after the 2016 election, in which "suburban women" were an important voting bloc, that "in general, if you were to pick one archetype," when politicians talk about suburban women, what they're actually talking about is "relatively educated and affluent whites" who live in relatively densely populated areas.[7]

The director of the Census Bureau freed us from the pressure of defining our terms completely. In a blog post in which he acknowledges the shortcomings of current definitions of our geographical regions, Robert Groves concludes: "Does that mean that there is no such thing as 'suburban' and 'rural'? No. It means there are many potential definitions for the terms, many of them best-suited for different uses."[8]

The important question to ask at this point is: How are we defining the terms for *our* uses in this conversation? I'm going to tell you how I'm using the terms. You can agree or disagree. But at least we'll all be on the same page. The events of my life take place, for the most part, in the following places:

- Bentonville, Arkansas (small town)
- Heflin, Louisiana (rural)
- Wheaton, Illinois (suburban)
- Conway, Arkansas (small city with a suburban "feel")
- Manhattan, New York (urban)

This range is helpful. Instead of having two points on a spectrum, with rural at one end and urban at the other, we have a web with several nodes. If we're asking questions like: What do these places have in common? How are they different? Is there any common cause between them?, then this range of places will help us make those kinds of distinctions. The chapters that follow focus primarily on rural Louisiana and small-town Arkansas, the sprawling Chicago suburbs, and urban New York.

Using these categories and data from several sources, we can distribute America's population in the following ways:

- As of the last census (2010), about 2 percent of the total US population lived in counties considered 100 percent rural

- 19 percent of the population lived in rural areas
- 54 percent of the population lived in a suburban area
- That left 27 percent living in urban areas
- Around 3.5 percent of the total US population lived in counties considered 100 percent urban

The landscape is complicated, and simplifying the picture for the sake of argument won't help matters. A better approach is to hold all this complexity together for the time being and see if we can't sort it out a bit as we go. We would do well to abandon the urban-versus-rural binary from the very beginning and be prepared for a more textured reality than we typically get from cable news and social media. We would do well to remember, too, that stronger than lexical definitions are connotations and mental images. In the end, definitions of "urban" and "rural" are like the Supreme Court's definition of obscenity: we know it when we see it.

3

Three Degrees of Separation

Bentonville, Arkansas

Kids know their hometown differently than grownups do. Kids know where all the broken boards are in all the fences. Kids know which deacons hide booze behind the pots and pans in their kitchen cabinets. Like their grownups, kids have a limited perspective on their hometowns. But, undistracted by bills and day jobs and HOA politics, kids see things differently.

From about middle school on, I saw Bentonville, Arkansas, by bicycle.

My friends and I were like the Goonies, minus the treasure hunting and the Italian crime family. We were like the gang from *Stranger Things* minus the fourth dimension. We rode our bikes to school in the mornings, across busy four-lane roads and open fields. After school, we explored back and side roads. In the late, long evenings of summer, we rode past neighbors changing the oil in their cars or rebuilding their carburetors in their driveways after work. On our way downtown, we pedaled past the Benton County Fairgrounds, which for most of the year was a large grassy lot in the middle of town. We rode on the street around "the square," as we called it, the historic downtown. The courthouse took up one side of it. (I spent some time there after an unfortunate series of speeding tickets in high school.) Opposite the courthouse a diner and Walton's Five and Dime. All the buildings faced the centerpiece: a small lawn that was home to a statue of a Confederate soldier. We never stopped in the square. There was nothing to do there. Instead we looked for open fields or construction sites to hunt for arrowheads turned up by backhoes.

For all the years I lived there—my entire childhood—Bentonville was a small town becoming larger. It was a growing island of civilization encircled by fields and forests. Widening roads and building new elementary schools and restaurants and housing subdivisions meant town and country overlapped in our city limits. Bentonville was home to the global headquarters of Walmart, the world's largest retailer. Cattle grazed in an open field across the street from our high school.

We felt a sense of isolation in the hills, not only from the rest of America but also from the rest of the state. Years after we were married, my wife pointed out to me, "When people ask you where you're from, you never say 'Arkansas.' You always say, '*Northwest* Arkansas.'" She's right. We felt culturally different in important ways from any of our neighbors, which I suppose heightened the sense that we had something worth protecting.

No one literally knew everyone, even though I sort of felt

like we did. I was good friends with the son of the chief of police and the man that ran the tire shop. A bank president and my barber and both of the town's veterinarians went to our church. My mom was a church secretary. It was easy to imagine that through those relationships I was probably connected to everyone else by no more than three degrees of separation. That's why it was best to say "yes, ma'am" and "no, ma'am" to every woman you met. Odds are if you didn't, news of your disrespect would make it back through the grapevine to your parents.

Sociologist Robert Wuthnow calls a town like this a "moral community." It's the kind of "place to which and in which people feel an obligation to one another and to uphold the local ways of being that govern their expectations about ordinary life and support their feelings of being at home and doing the right things."[1] Even if everyone doesn't *actually* know everyone, we could all share the sentiment that we knew what everyone valued and that we held those values in common.

An important part of the expectation that we shared in common, at least in the subset of the community I knew well, was church. Our church was one of the historic churches near the square with all the other "First" churches—First Baptist, First United Methodist, First Presbyterian. Our first chapel (what we called the "old sanctuary") was built in the 1800s. Church was the sun around which my life orbited from early elementary school until I left home for college. For a number of years I was at church six days a week and sometimes more. My mom was a secretary at the church, and during one season of childhood I rode my bike to the church building after school and stayed there for the last couple of hours of every business day. On Wednesday nights we stayed late for dinner in the fellowship hall where we ate lots of open-faced sandwiches, followed by a prayer meeting for Mom and Royal Ambassadors for me. We were frequently the first people and the last people in the large, dark church building, labyrinthine from years of renovation and additions.

It seemed to me that church exerted considerable influence on daily life in Bentonville and not only upon the lives of those who attended worship somewhere. I played baseball in the spring and there were rarely practices on Wednesday evenings, as Wednesdays were set apart for church services. There were never games on Sundays. In fact, there was a lot you couldn't do on Sundays. You had to leave the county to buy gas on a Sunday; you had to leave the *state* (just one county north) to buy liquor any day of the week. Benton County, like more than half the counties in Arkansas, was a dry county. Of course I had friends whose families didn't attend church anywhere. But I knew they were *good* people who agreed about the local ways of being and doing the right things. It never occurred to me they might have different values. Maybe we just spent our Sunday mornings and Wednesday evenings differently.

And while all of this was true during any one frozen moment of time in my childhood, it is equally true that our town was changing. The decade or so that I was in school was a season of remarkable growth. The population nearly doubled between 1990 and 2000, from 12,021 to 20,413. The population has more than doubled again since then to almost 50,000, but that's a story for later. Growth meant people from surrounding towns were moving in to Bentonville, for sure. It also meant that people from all over the country were moving into town. New people threatened our sense that everyone knew everyone and that we all shared basically the same values and interests. Radical change is a real threat to a moral community, especially when it feels as if it is imposed by outside forces or when citizens feel powerless to stop it. A fundamental change that results in people questioning whether their new neighbors share their values and agree about what's good and right requires more than adjusting habits. It requires an entirely new orientation to your town. It makes you an outsider where yesterday you were an insider. As our population swelled, our moral community was in decline.

Enemies Foreign

Our church made changes to adapt to our changing community. We abandoned traditional worship for contemporary. We went from meeting in the gym to constructing a new, impressive worship space. And the church grew. But I internalized a deep concern that, while there were signs of life and health in the foreground, danger lurked beyond the horizon. The great threat to our values and way of life, our freedom to worship and discipline our children as we saw fit, was secular liberalism that came from out of town. I grew up with a tangible sense of fear that the freedoms and advantages we enjoyed and the relative piety we all shared could be taken from us by forces outside of us. Of primary concern were federal judges in Washington or in our own state capital hundreds of miles away. Voting the right people into the right offices was an important measure for stemming the tide of godless humanism. In light of these forces, and the growing numbers of newcomers who arrived with different interests and values, a major theme in my small-town childhood was resistance.

Resistance was led, in my case, by the church. I was part of the furniture there. I knew every inch of that building, including the roof, to which I sometimes escaped during Royal Ambassadors meetings. Faith became important to me in my later teens. Before and until then, *church* was important. The church in a small and growing town shaped how I understood my place in the world. It shaped my posture not only toward my classmates but also toward my teachers, education, and information in general, and to the broader culture outside the church and its gravitational pull. It determined the fronts on which we waged the resistance.

The place we felt the pressure of urban liberalism upon our small town the strongest was in school. Until 1968, an Arkansas statute prohibited teaching human evolution in public schools. (This was more than forty years after a teacher named John Scopes was tried and found guilty and fired in Tennessee for teaching human evolution, in violation of a similar statute.) Then in 1968, the US Supreme Court ruled the Arkansas statute unconstitutional in *Epperson v. Arkansas*. After this ruling, some parts of Arkansas passed laws requiring teachers to teach both creation science *and* human evolution—and to clarify that evolution was *one theory* among others and not established fact—until 1987, when that practice was struck down as unconstitutional.

I didn't know any of this. But knowing it now makes a lot of sense of some of my experiences as a boy in school. It was with a sense of dread that we aged toward high school biology. Parents knew the sequence of courses. Ninth grade was physical science—dirt and rocks and stuff. Tenth grade was chemistry—no risk of evolution there. Eleventh grade was biology—there's the problem. I recall sincere people debating whether children should walk out in protest when evolution was taught. I remember feeling compelled to clarify, when my teacher discussed the science of evolution, that evolution was, in fact, a *theory*. It was a point of faithful discipleship to stand firm for creation against secular humanist advance.

To corroborate my memory, I put out a request on Facebook asking people if they remembered this being a thing. I asked:

> I have strong memories of being in science class in junior high and high school and feeling morally obligated to resist lessons about evolution. I don't remember if my church leaders advised us to resist it, or if I put that pressure on myself. I'm curious how other people experienced this.

By Monday the post had elicited more than a hundred comments. The question clearly struck a nerve. There was enough feedback to verify anecdotally that I'm remembering the past more or less accurately on this point. Folks with evangelical backgrounds from across the country, most of them from rural places, remember being prepared in youth groups, especially, to stand up for the truth in their science class.

There were two problems with evolution. First, it strained common sense. One friend who responded to my Facebook question replied that she still rolls her eyes "at the millions of years old thing." A pastor I respected taught me this little poem to confirm the ridiculousness of evolutionary theory:

> Once he was an amoeba swimming in a pond.
> Then he was a tadpole with a tail stuck on.
> Next he was a monkey swinging in a tree.
> Now he's a professor with a PhD.

The other problem with evolution is that it undermined the basic tenet of God's direct and ongoing activity in the world. It reduced us all to a random collection of atoms and eliminated intention. There was a more spiritual way to read the natural world. A friend of my dad's asked me once if I knew why robins had red breasts. I didn't.

"It's because robins were the birds that plucked the thorns from Jesus's brow after he died on the cross. Before then, robins had white breasts. Ever since, they're blood red."

I knew enough at the time to know this isn't how genetics worked. I didn't know enough at the time to question whether robins lived in first-century Palestine. Nor did I know enough to suspect he was passing on a bit of heartwarming mythology totally unaware. His face was so sincere—I can see it clearly still—that even though I doubted him, I was convinced he believed it.

Later in school it became a matter of discipleship to

excuse myself from reading certain books in English class. Mostly this was because the books contained adult language (words I'm sure we all heard on prime time television—there were gaps in our resistance), and this violated my religious convictions. Other books and poetry contained adult themes, and we were allowed by our school and encouraged by our parents to abstain for conscience's sake.

Resisting evolution didn't bother me much. I like animals and being outdoors but had little natural curiosity for the contents of our biology textbook. I did, however, feel some inner turmoil about taking my stand against inappropriate reading material. From an early age, and especially by high school, I was an avid reader. I loved that you could travel a million miles in a book without ever leaving home. I loved encountering new cultures and customs and exploring new ideas in stories. Saying no to good fiction, even on religious grounds, created an internal tension for me.

Nevertheless we, in our small classrooms, in our own small town in the Bible Belt, were prepared to be foot soldiers in the culture war. Whether or not there was actually a war going on is hard to say. One friend commented, "I distinctly remember waiting for a venomous attack on my beliefs from the 'world' that never really came."

That's how I remember it, too. We were outfitted for battle and warned of an impending onslaught of liberal hoards. But in our small, conservative town, they never came. Now that I think of it, the intellectual gestapo that we feared was a bit like the agents we feared would one day go house to house collecting our firearms. We were convinced that there was a global coordinated effort to undermine our faith and brain-wash our children. We weren't going to take it sitting down.

Enemies Domestic

A second important threat to our way of life came from within our community. As I recall, the devout and wayward alike assumed God existed and that He sent people either to heaven or hell. We agreed about common decency and basic morality. But all that could change in a generation, if good God-fearing people backslid and allowed unbelief to take hold.

Unbelief wasn't a starting point in my mind. It was a destination that someone could reach only after willfully rejecting the faith we all shared. In my view, everyone was essentially backslidden and didn't need to be convinced of the truth of Christianity so much as they needed to be reminded of it. The only real pagans in America lived on her coasts, where moral corruption and spiritual regression had metastasized and affected all of urban or Northern culture. Their influence was headed our way. It had been headed our way for a while. Back in the 1940s, an evangelist named Harry Black wrote a series of talks for young people on the dangers of all sorts of youth culture staples, from playing cards to listening to jazz music. In one article about the dangers of immodest dress, Black reflects on the origins of these immodest styles. "Where do we get all these godless and 'sex appeal' styles?" he asked. "From New York. And where do they get them? From Paris. And where does Paris get them? From the devil!"[2] That summarized my sense of things exactly. We lived three degrees of separation from hell. The only protection was total spiritual vigilance at all times.

We knew our battle was not against flesh and blood alone, but against spiritual powers bent on leading our own faithful astray and preventing others from joining the faith. So in addition to general resistance against evolution and the like, we also coordinated more asserted attacks on spiritual darkness.

The great coup was co-opting Halloween, a spiritually dark ordeal, as an opportunity to share with our neighbors the good news of the saving work of Jesus. This we did for a number of years at our church through an experience we called the Hereafter House. It was known by other names, such as Hell House, elsewhere. The event was a guided tour through Heaven and Hell designed to remind our neighbors of their options for eternity: smoking or nonsmoking. The tour began with Lucifer welcoming guests while disguised as an angel of light: dressed in a business suit and talking smooth about the promise of worldly pleasures. From there the group toured Hell, which was illuminated by black light. What I remember most vividly is the floor in Hell covered in packing peanuts sprayed with fluorescent paint that, under the black light, made convincing hot coals.

The tour through Hell involved a series of vignettes that dramatized the futility of a life spent indulging in sinful pleasures. There was the cheating husband, the drunk, the charlatan. One year featured a teen drunk-driving car accident. That one was a crowd pleaser. One friend was killed on impact and sent straight to her fiery doom. She pleaded with the visitors to warn her still-living friends of the futility and dangers of waywardness. As she spoke, two diabolical henchmen dragged a new inmate through the crowd kicking and screaming and tossed her into the coals. The young woman speaking is horrified to see her new cellmate is one of those friends she wanted us to warn—she was too late. Another teen dead at the scene.

And that, kids, is why you shouldn't drink and drive.

One year the drunk teen was played exceedingly convincingly. Her thrashing through the crowd was truly terrifying; her weeping in the hot coals of Hell was Oscar-worthy; her quiet sobbing and moaning after the scene sold the authenticity. When the tour was over we discovered she had actually broken her arm in the tussle with Satan's jailors. This became critical youth group lore for some time. All the cool kids wanted to play in Hell.

This sort of production has either recently made a comeback or never went away. Either way, national news outlets have recently taken notice. The journey through Hell has been updated to connect with the times. A recent Hell House in Texas featured a shouting match between Trump supporters and Black Lives Matter activists. All the modern commentary on these programs emphasizes how the Hell House experiences demonstrate evangelical politics. They're right, of course. But that's not how I experienced it. I figured it was all about morality. There's a fine line between morality and politics, as is clear in the frequent treatment of abortion in Hell Houses.[3]

As I remember it, our version of the experience was not particularly graphic. I don't remember any bloody suicides or abortion procedures, which are reportedly part of some events. Nevertheless, from a dramatic perspective, all the kids thought Hell was well done. Teenagers always wanted to volunteer in Hell, writhing, moaning, and shrieking or sitting dazed with their hand over a bleeding head wound—for the glory of God.

The harrowing final monologue in Hell was given by the "good person" who did all the right things and lived a virtuous life, who attended church and tithed and all that, but who never truly made Jesus Lord of their life. No blood or gore. Just good, old-fashioned self-righteousness.

At the end of the tour Satan reappears, this time exposed in his true form. To our credit I believe we eschewed horns and hooves and tail and opted instead for general creepiness. While he was making his final appeals for a life of sin, a heavenly being of some sort led folks upstairs into the bright and glittering and air-conditioned acreage of Heaven.

For a number of reasons, there were age requirements for serving in Hell. There were the logistics of transportation to and from late-night rehearsals and performances; certainly, that privileged actors of driving age. There was the general optics of a child in Hell that we probably wanted to avoid, as well as niggling thoughts about an age of accountability. This precluded anyone under age thirteen, to be safe.

Because I was at the church every day anyway, I got to help prepare the Hellscape after school for the weeks leading up to Halloween one year. I spray-painted packing peanuts, erected the cells for wayward sinners, and strung black lights. As a preteen I would have loved the opportunity to serve in the underworld. But Heaven is where I made my kingdom contribution.

Heaven, as I remember it, was less engaging of the senses. It was a wedding chapel, our "old sanctuary," draped in white. Soft music played and there were mansions of gold—painted one year by my Granddaddy—in the background. The citizens of Heaven wore white baptismal robes and gave brief testimonies, I'm sure, about their lives on earth and the grace of God. There were deathbed confessions of faith as well as the lifelong faithful. At least one teen from the aforementioned car accident made it to Heaven each year. She made bad life choices but was sincerely saved nonetheless.

But I was the showstopper.

I had a part that was both theologically and politically significant. Before a crowd of our townies and classmates, I stepped out on my cloud each evening for a week and said:

"I came to heaven as a baby when my mother chose to have an abortion."

This is the only line I remember. There must have been others. There must have been some explanation, drawn from extrabiblical sources, regarding why I was now ten or eleven years old. Who cares? I was the emotional crescendo in our small-town performance. The argument for which there is no counterargument.

Baby-Back Ribs and the Root of All Evil

It turns out that those who feared that life as we knew it in our small town would soon be over were not totally off the mark. When I started school in the late 1980s, Bentonville was what Dante Chinni and James Gimpel, authors of *Our*

Patchwork Nation, would describe as an "Evangelical Epi-center." Evangelical epicenters are whiter than the general population, more likely to vote Republican, and more likely to attend evangelical churches. They are committed to "holding the line against whatever changes threaten to transform the country in ways they believe are for the worse."[4]

Before I had graduated high school, though, there was evidence of change. Previously the seat of a dry county, Bentonville had started distributing liquor licenses to restaurants. Chili's was one of the first casual restaurant chains to open a location in Bentonville. I heard rumors that the reason there was enough popular support for the liquor license was because so many new people had moved into town from other places, people who didn't share our values. Maybe so. Maybe our appetites overwhelmed our convictions. The heart wants what the heart wants, after all. Maybe our hearts wanted baby-back ribs.

In my senior year of high school I visited a friend's house. He belonged to a Christian family that had relocated to Bentonville from another state. Hanging out in their kitchen one evening, I discovered a new piece of kitchen equipment I had never seen before. It was a tall metal cylinder with a hole in the middle: a wine chiller. Around the opening where you inserted the bottle were engraved a few words from Scripture. They weren't the biblical words I usually associated with wine. It didn't say, "Wine is a mocker, strong drink a brawler" (Prov. 20:1). It didn't say, "Do not look at wine when it is red, when it sparkles in the cup and goes down smoothly" (Prov. 23:31).

It read, "Use a little wine for thy stomach's sake" (1 Tim. 5:23 KJV).

Friends of mine viewed our small and growing town differently. Some of us took on the mantle of resistance as a long-term commitment. Some of us knew the airwaves and our textbooks were full of fake news, and the radical call of discipleship was to ignore it or silence it.

That was me. I was headed to college prepared to resist and mistrust any source of information associated with the secular liberal worldview. I couldn't have told you how the pieces fit together, but I knew evolution and abortion and sexual transgression were all pieces in the puzzle.

This is why no one had to tell me to destroy all my secular music or to encourage my classmates to do the same. For a few weeks in high school, we collected cassettes and CDs by secular musicians, VHS tapes and DVDs of movies with questionable content, and other strongholds in our lives. We collected these items on the stage in our youth worship space, a box we called the "sin bin." When it was full, we organized a bonfire and burned the box, which we could only assume made a pleasing aroma to the Lord. This is why no one had to encourage me to wear Christian T-shirts or bracelets or necklaces that might spark an evangelistic conversation with a spiritual seeker. It's why no one had to pressure us to organize an after party for prom, where we might successfully avoid fornicating.

It's why some of us kissed dating goodbye and why we learned to make a case for Christ. It's why even the best of us feared we might be left behind.

It's why some of us kissed dating goodbye and why we

learned to make a case for Christ. It's why even the best of us feared we might be left behind.

Other friends of mine responded differently. Some of my closest friends left. Some of them never looked back. They found the moral community stifling. Some found the unique pressures of living in the Christian subculture to be too strong to bear.

Years later I, too, rejected many of the idiosyncrasies of my small-town Christian raising. But it took a long while. And I never felt the same need to flee that some of my close friends felt. One factor that may have shifted the balance for me is that I always had an escape, an ever-present release valve. It was the country.

Fishing in the creek on summer days. Long weekend hunting trips to the deer lease. Summers with my grandparents in Louisiana. These times and places were a refuge for me. Instead of making my world smaller, retreating to rural America broadened my perspective and may have saved my faith.

4

Making Life Imaginable

Heflin, Louisiana
Zachary, Louisiana

As soon as school and my Little League baseball season were over for the summer, I headed south each year to spend several weeks with my grandparents, on both sides, in Louisiana.

The drive south took us down from the rugged Ozark Mountains of Northwest Arkansas, through the flat hardwood bottoms on the west side of the state and into the sandy-earthed, pine-forested coastal plain region that bordered Louisiana. In terms of distance, it wasn't far—just a couple hundred miles. Culturally, though, it was a journey from the South to the Deep South. The climate was hotter and sticky with humidity. From about age ten I wore glasses, and the lenses fogged up every time I stepped outside of the air-conditioned car or house. That never happened at home in Bentonville. Populations were different, too. Northwest Arkansas was almost entirely white. Louisiana was more diverse. Even though I experienced rural life all year, on weekends or during hunting trips with my dad, the most concentrated dose of rural life I experienced was in the summers. My rural experiences were different from my small-town experiences in important ways. In the first place, while both sides of my family were devoutly Christian, my summers contained relatively little explicitly Christian activity. One notable exception was the summer my grandma tried to help me learn to speak in tongues.

We both gave it our best shot. It wasn't in the cards.

In any case, the summers for me were a break from the culture wars.

At Grandmother and Granddaddy's, my mother's parents, I passed long, hot days fishing, building, exploring, knee-deep and barefoot in Lake Bistineau, with water brown as strong iced tea. Once or twice a week we'd go to town (occasionally for church on Wednesday evenings and always on Sunday mornings), a twenty-minute drive down rural highways bleached and cracked by the sun. It was on those highways that I learned to drive.

Grandmother taught me in her old Buick LaCrosse when I was ten or eleven. Her philosophy was that I was a safe driving height when I was taller than she was, and because she is five feet tall, I reached that milestone fairly early. Once we had pulled off the main road onto Lake Road on our way home from town, she'd stop the car and we'd swap seats. I drove home the rest of the way.

"The speed limit is a *maximum* speed, not a *mandatory* speed," she told me often. "Just because it says 45 miles per hour doesn't mean you have to go that fast."

She needn't worry. I was cautious. So cautious that when oncoming traffic approached I eased onto the shoulder to make sure everyone had plenty of room. When my Granddaddy was in the car, he'd say, "It's smoother on the road."

He didn't share my grandmother's view of speed limits, either. When I drove too slowly with him in the car, he'd say, "You may find it easier to steer a *moving* vehicle."

From the outside looking in, we were a preteen boy and his tiny grandmother cruising a Buick land yacht well below the speed limit. From my perspective in the driver's seat, I was experiencing the great American freedom of the automobile. And "freedom" was the watchword of my rural experience.

Most of the time I spent with them, we passed at the lake. Some mornings we woke early to fish. We motored away from the pier through a forest of slender, straight cypress trees in the eerie quiet of predawn. Gradually the air turned gray, then golden, as the sun rose over the lake. It shone silver through hanging Spanish moss. On breezy mornings, the moss fluttered like curtains in an open window. If I fished with Granddaddy we might boat a long way before stopping in one of the fishing holes named for successful fishermen of previous generations—places with names like Skinner's Slough or Roy Rhone's Slough. If I went fishing alone, I had to stay near enough to the shore that I could hear Grandmother whistle and whistle back to let her know I was alright. My mother's mental image of me during these years was red-faced, sweaty, and grimy and—when I was very young—with pockets full of small fish that I caught and kept as souvenirs.

Good Country People

On the mornings we didn't fish early, we slept in and worked around the house instead. Grandmother scrambled eggs and fried bacon. She kept me full to the brim all summer long. And I was Granddaddy's right-hand man. As I got older, he saved big jobs around the house until I was there to help. One summer we laid the cinder block footing for an addition on the cabin. Another year I helped him dig in the hot sand to excavate the old septic system so we could replace it with a new one. It was slow, sweaty work—Granddaddy's specialty. The old pipes bent and twisted in strange ways, turning when they should have run straight. We were sure by the time we had them all uncovered the pipes would spell:

SUCKERS

He could have paid someone to do these things, I suppose. But part of good living was being able to do it on your own. From their rural upbringing, my grandparents inherited and passed down to me through such experiences a deep self-reliance and resourcefulness. Sociologist Robert Wuthnow characterizes this value as "ingenuity," and it was an important trait throughout rural America from the 1950s on, celebrated in farm journals and literature about country life. "An ingenious person in these accounts was someone with imagination, given to new ideas, and yet a nonexpert who used simple skills, tinkered, poked around, puttered, and came up with a device that was cheap, time saving, practical, and easy to understand."[1] A friend of mine who grew up in Arkansas and lives in California recently described the same value in simpler terms. One of his friends dated several men but says she is through with "California boys" and is now looking for a rural Southern man. My friend asked her why. "I guess I just want a man who knows how to solve a problem without spending money," she said.

That's a good description of the value of resourcefulness I internalized during summers with my grandparents. They could stretch a dollar so thin you could see through it. But I didn't think of it as a value so much as a necessity. It was a thirty-minute drive from the lake to the nearest hardware store. It is best to use the right tool for the job, but often you can't. So we made do. This wasn't duct tape and super glue winging it. But we got creative. Even today I attribute my approach to problem solving and my sense that no task is too large to attempt—nothing a clever man can't handle with a little thinking and a little hard work—to these rural experiences.

A Kinder Look on Culture

The summers were not all semi-feral exploring and wholesome rural fun. My grandparents on both sides exposed me to more culture, from Louisiana folk culture to so-called "high culture," than I encountered at home. Granddaddy retired young, almost as long ago as I can remember. Instead of spending those years, which turned into decades, puttering around the house, they first studied French so they could take a long-anticipated trip to Europe. One summer Granddaddy grew a pencil-thin mustache for effect and Grandmother experimented with French cuisine to lend authenticity to their class meetings. After French they took tae kwon do. Granddaddy was already a painter, and when days got too hot for fishing or building, we'd sit on the sun porch for the afternoon and draw and paint and listen to Grandmother's records. Some of them I play for my kids now, including a 1963 recording of "Peter and the Wolf" narrated by Sterling Holloway, who also voiced Winnie the Pooh. The opening seconds of that record—"This is the story of . . . uh . . . Peter and the Wolf"—send me back to rural Louisiana twenty-five years ago.

Grandmother taught voice and piano before retirement and had an enormous collection of classical and big band vinyl albums. Their collection of secular music and art books full of nudes, their interest in French culture for its own sake, and their persistent intellectual curiosity all felt mildly transgressive by the standards of my small-town religiosity.

Our time together developed a sacred rhythm: early mornings fishing or a big breakfast—always with bacon. We worked in the cool morning hours and took Dr. Pepper breaks when we got hot and tired. We watched birds through binoculars and identified unfamiliar species using a well-worn field guide. Then it was back to work in the afternoon. For years this rhythm shaped my view of the good life.

My other grandparents, Grandpa and Grandma, lived further south and east in Louisiana, in a sleepy town near Baton Rouge. The drive to their house led through cotton fields, past miles of flat farmland and, briefly, through the kudzu-covered banks of Natchez, Mississippi. It was a journey deeper into the Deep South, into the French south. Their house sat among centuries-old pecan trees in what used to be a plantation. Time at their house was more cosmopolitan. Grandma cooked wonderfully. Originally from Minnesota, she had a lifetime's recipes from her Northern heritage. But from my earliest memory she had mastered Cajun and Creole staples: étouffée and jambalaya and red beans and rice. The textures and flavors and, in general, her great cooking made me an adventurous eater. Her efforts to make me a *healthy* eater were less successful. She ate organic and free-range decades before the trend took hold nationwide. One time she fried a pan of bacon and left the fat to harden in the pan. When it was cool she called me in to show it to me.

"This is what eating bacon does to your arteries," she said.

I preferred my other grandmother's approach to breakfast.

Grandpa worked for most of my childhood, so I spent less time with him during the day. But his impact came in the form of books and conversation. He was always reading—novels and nonfiction and newspapers. And he was always eager to talk about what he was reading. He was my only family member who read voraciously. Together, they took me to zoos and monuments and museums, to roadside restaurants that served Creole cuisine and featured live zydeco music, so I could learn to dance the regional dance. We toured reconstructed pioneer villages, art museums, and antebellum homes. We encountered new cultures and foreign languages.

These experiences planted in me a deep appreciation for

the American experience, the history and heritage of both the rural industrious poor and the rural creative classes. If my home church and town experience encouraged me to resist new things and culture, my summers in rural Louisiana celebrated intellectual curiosity, creative expression, local culture, and new experiences. Was this a "typical" rural experience? I don't know. It was mine. And my grandparents'. And their families' before them. So while it may have been unique to *me*, it was not unique to us.

If my home church and town experience encouraged me to resist new things and culture, my summers in rural Louisiana celebrated intellectual curiosity, creative expression, local culture, and new experiences.

My grandfolks may have lamented the nation's moral decline in quiet voices while they washed the dishes at night. I never heard them. Instead my time in rural Louisiana gave me a much more affirming perspective on culture and the arts. My grandparents showed me faithful Christians who loved the arts, danced, and celebrated local culture through good food.

It was thrilling.

Old Time Religion

My summertime rural experience also exposed me to different forms of Christian experience. To begin with, life in Bentonville gave me very little practice navigating cross-cultural relationships. The year I graduated high school, my hometown of Bentonville, Arkansas, was slightly more than 90 percent white, less than 1 percent black, and about 4 percent "other."[2] The most significant increase in the nonwhite "other" population was among Latin American, particularly Mexican, immigrants. The growth was more dramatic in neighboring towns, and it was dramatic enough that my high school soccer team played one nearby school whose team was almost entirely Spanish-speaking. I recall the coach losing his patience about the fact that he couldn't communicate with his team and screaming, "Speak English, will ya?!" from the sidelines.

The influx of Spanish speaking immigrants sparked a bit of a panic in town. One friend of mine lived on a farm outside city limits. There was lots of property for sale between my house and his. On one drive out to their place, we passed real estate signs that included the term "Primo." His mom was convinced that this term was a Spanish code word to attract Mexicans and leave hapless white folks in the dark. Of course I believed her.

The word is Italian and is slang for "top quality."

Then and now, Arkansas was unevenly diverse.[3] North of central Arkansas and the state capitol, populations are almost entirely white with pockets of growing diversity. In the center of the state, south, and especially east, there are larger populations of ethnic minorities. My interaction with different kinds of people could have been different if I'd grown up elsewhere in our small state. But I didn't.

The ethnic landscape was very different in Louisiana where my grandparents lived. In the year I graduated high school, the town nearest one set of grandparents, Minden,

Louisiana, was about 45 percent white and more than 50 percent black.[4] Zachary, Louisiana, where my other grandparents lived, was about 70 percent white and about 30 percent black.[5] The suburb they lived in was segregated—mostly white in a county that was about half white. But church was integrated. And it was exciting.

My home church had already abandoned the organ, but their church was years into the future of contemporary worship. They had electric guitars and a New Orleans–style horn section. The church was full of black folks and white folks—something I had never experienced. Worshipers were enthusiastic, even ecstatic. They danced and sweated. They spoke in tongues. And there were thousands of them. They were a sea of dancing, shouting, Holy Ghost–filled Christians.

We were all washed in the same blood, but they were "more than conquerors."

We were saved, but they were overcomers.

We believed in Jesus, but they claimed promises, addressed the devil, and bound the strongman. It was somehow both more mystical and more practical than the faith I experienced at home.

It was a vision, too, of a life of integrated worship which I never saw anywhere else until I was an adult. I don't remember any social interactions with black people. But I remember dancing, singing, holding hands, and being hugged by black worshipers.

This was the sum total of my cross-cultural experience until adulthood. It was a peek at both a different kind of Christianity and different kinds of Christians. While back home we spent our worship service wringing our hands about the creeping cancer of secular humanism, they were being slain in the Spirit and evidencing a depth of celebration I wasn't accustomed to seeing at church.

Sitting till Bedtime

Despite the geographical isolation of my grandparents' house, we nevertheless enjoyed the hospitality of rural community and the fellowship of neighbors. Some lived nearby and some far away. My grandparents checked on elderly neighbors to make sure they were well and as often as not dropped off a tin of home-baked treats. We sat on the porch of the neighbor's house in the long shadows of late summer to shell bushel baskets full of purple-hull peas until our fingers were stained violet. On especially hot days and in the evenings after supper, we hosted church friends or distant relations for card games and long, late nights of visiting. Wendell Berry describes a local practice in his home state of Kentucky known as "sitting till bedtime," in which neighbors snacked and "told each other stories . . . that they had all heard before." The stories were an important form of identity formation. "Sometimes they told stories about each other, about themselves, living again in their own memories and thus keeping their memories alive."[6]

The stories the grownups told around card tables in the summer reinforced the sense that during my free-range summers, at least, I was participating in a family tradition of good, clean, old-fashioned fun. That working with my hands and spending hours and days in solitude in the sticky, hot sun was a birthright of sorts. Grandmother and Granddaddy told me stories about friends and family cutting class to spend a long weekend camping on Lake Bistineau. About trying to harvest honey from an ancient hive in a tree we called the "bee tree"—stories that ended (in my remembering of them) with nude, welt-covered boys diving into the oily-black water for safety from angry bees. About exploding lanterns and missing eyebrows. About tipping outhouses and good-natured battles using waterlogged corncobs as projectiles. About sliding a 2x6 board under the seat of an old Model T so the whole gang had a place to sit when the kids took the car for a joy ride. The great American freedom of the automobile that I experienced was an experience my grandparents and aunts and uncles enjoyed, too, years before.

The cumulative effect of it all was that it created in me a deep sense of connection to my family and to those people who were important to my family, even if they were relative strangers to me. This network was especially evident in a crisis. The lake house has flooded twice in my lifetime. Both times neighbors joined forces to rip out drywall and pull up carpet and ferry furniture by boat to dry ground. You may save your own place first, but you always help out.

A deep sense of neighborly connection extended beyond the present and backward into the past. Grandmother's house was full of artifacts that reinforced a feeling of connection to our ancestry. She was the family archivist. Her magnum opus for most of my childhood was organizing, labeling, and scrapbooking several shoe boxes worth of old photos that spanned many generations. At least once a summer we leafed through the progress in her album since the last time I was there or thumbed through the boxes of still unorganized photos. She patiently reminded me how I was related to everyone in the pictures. She often fell silent looking at them, her fingers gently on the pages. I understood that these images connected us with an important heritage.

In shadow boxes around the house, in bedrooms and bathrooms and other places, Grandmother tidily displayed small personal treasures: perfume bottles emptied long ago that Granddaddy brought her from his travels during the Korean War, music boxes, and figurines carved by her brother. There were a couple pieces of furniture made by Grandmother's father, whom we called Daddy Carl. He made a houseful of furniture out of lumber salvaged from shipping crates at the ammo plant where he worked. The mementos were not dead artifacts; they are living icons that connect us with a deep history and tradition. Grandmother took them often from the shelf and told their stories—who made them and when, where they were purchased and why, what compelled her to keep them all these years. Grandmother brought them to life for me with her loving touch.

If "resistance" was a central theme during the school year at home, "freedom" was another, and the center of my rural experience. But the summers intensified all my small-town and rural experience and planted deep longings for solitude and self-sufficiency. The good life, as I internalized it, consisted of space to think and act as I please, without much external interference. The furniture of the good life was guns and boats and knives and old shoes you could wear in the water. It was Dr. Pepper and playing cards and old records and binoculars.

The stories the grown-ups told together with my own experiences reinforced a deep sense that my childhood, while different in important ways, was an awful lot like my grandparents' childhoods. Swap out an early-'90s model Buick for a Model T and our stories of underage driving and lake expeditions were essentially the same. There were only small differences between tipping outhouses and digging up septic tanks. We had a heritage to share and pass down and preserve. Of all the places that have influenced me, the summertime South was *the* place. *My* place. I had the deep sense that it was the way it always had been, and I would have fought hard to resist any changes that would ruin it.

Making Life Imaginable

Author Wendell Berry explained that when he read *Huckleberry Finn* for the first time, the book "made my boyhood imaginable to me in a way that it otherwise would not have been."[7] On one level Berry meant that Huck Finn validated his own desire to escape school and church and revel in the outdoors—a desire that earned him a reputation for being "bad," even in his rural hometown. In a deeper sense, though, the character Huck Finn gave Berry a "comforting sense of precedent." It gave him the sense that his behavior and proclivities *belonged* in a real way to the world he lived in, even when schoolmarms and church ladies punished him for them. The novel helped him find his continuity (real or imagined) with his ancestry. "And later," he explains,

> It helped me to make my grandfather's boyhood in Port
> Royal [Kentucky] imaginable to me. Still later, when I
> had come to some knowledge of literature and history,
> I saw that that old green book [Huckleberry Finn] had,
> fairly early, made imaginable to me my family's life as in-
> habitants of the great river system to which we, like Mark
> Twain, belonged. The world my grandfather had grown
> up in, in the [eighteen] eighties and nineties, was not
> greatly changed from the world of Mark Twain's boyhood
> in the thirties and forties. And the vestiges of that world
> had not entirely passed away by the time of my own boy-
> hood in the thirties and forties of the next century.[8]

My grandparents on both sides gave me a "comforting
sense of precedent" in their love for the slow and remote rural
South. They gave it, too, in the sense that my artistic and lit-
erary bent felt out of place at times in my cultural context.
But never with them. Painting with Granddaddy; discussing
books with Grandpa; singing with Grandmother and hearing
stories about the importance of music in her childhood; and
cooking family recipes with Grandma provided a "comforting
sense of precedent" that these people who embodied many
typical rural and small-town Southern values—resourcefulness, independence, solitude, and neighborliness—also tran-
scended the simple stereotypes of rural people as uncultured
or unrefined.

They gave me a sense of precedent for admiring my

cultural heritage and, at the same time, exploring beyond it to experience and incorporate new things. They helped me see dimensions of our heritage that are fundamental to rural culture but frequently unnoticed by outsiders—the importance of storytelling, music, and beauty in its many forms. And they made imaginable to me that these values, in this balance, were my birthright from generations past.

The Kind of Place You Leave

"We gotta get out while we're young."

—Bruce Springsteen, "*Born to Run*"[1]

America can't decide how it feels about its rural and small-town parts.

On the one hand, our poets and politicians have waxed eloquent about the simple virtues of rural life for more than a hundred years. At least since Henry David Thoreau spent two years in a simple cabin by Walden Pond, Americans have sensed that to truly live life the way we were meant to live it, you have to leave behind the distractions of civilization and engage nature in spare simplicity. "I went to the woods because I wished to live deliberately," Thoreau begins, in his 1854 account of his rural experiment. He wanted "to live deep and suck out all the marrow of life,"[2] he said. He could only do that, he believed, by retreating from society into the wild. In addition to poets seeking life to the full, our rural places were home to frontiersmen and pioneers who tamed the West and crossed snow-capped mountains in search of the American dream.

Others around the same time had a less romantic view of frontier life. A journalist named George M. Weston used 1850 census data to summarize the condition of poor white people in the American South. The majority of them "retire to the outskirts of civilization," he observed, "where they lead a semi-savage life, sinking deeper and more hopelessly into barbarism with each succeeding generation." Weston believed they would be better off if they moved into industrial cities, where "the general average of education and intelligence is raised by the facilities afforded by density of population."[3]

One historian summarizes America's divided perception of rural places in this way:

> In his most favorable cast as backwoodsman, he was a homespun philosopher, an independent spirit, and a strong and courageous man who shunned fame and wealth. But turn him over and he became the white savage, a ruthless brawler and eye-gouger. This unwholesome type lived a brute existence in a dingy log cabin, with yelping dogs at his heels, a haggard wife, and a mongrel brood of brown and yellow brats to complete the sorry scene.[4]

By the early twentieth century, intellectuals in America were betraying a clear bias in favor of city life. Sociologist Edward Ross set out in 1905 to classify all human beings into "four types of intellect" and identify where in America the different types are most likely to be found. The *lowest type* of intellect "has few ideas." They are rural people that congregate "about seaboard and lakeboard, in all the mountain regions, and on the great plains." On *the next rung up* are folks who enjoy "safe, commonplace, profitable occupations." They are kind but intellectually dull. They make up a quarter of the population and "predominate in the South." The third type are principled and hardworking, make up about 20 percent of the population, and can be found from New England through the Midwest. The highest type is "marked by breadth and balance, clear perceptions, sound judgment, careful reasoning, and critical thinking." They are the minority —making up just 1.5 percent of the population. They are found "here and there *in cities.*"[5]

At this point in history, the rural people these commentators had in mind were most likely the sort of solitary wilderness dwellers we think of as squatters or pioneers. That is, these commentators weren't necessarily talking about farmers in small communities across the heartland.

And for that reason it is all the more remarkable that the legendary Baltimore journalist H. L. Mencken made an interesting move in the 1920s when he broadened the stereotype of the ignorant woodsman to include the citizens of small-town Dayton, Tennessee. Mencken traveled from Baltimore to Dayton in 1925 to cover the trial of John T. Scopes, a substitute high school teacher who was charged with teaching human evolution in violation of local statute. Mencken could hardly believe the resistance. And so in his reporting of the Scopes Trial in 1925, he commented not only on the court proceedings but also on the general tone and tenor of life in small-town Dayton.

At first, the newsman was impressed by the condition of the town. "The town, I confess, greatly surprised me," he wrote to his urban audience. "I expected to find a squalid Southern village, with . . . pigs rooting under the houses and the inhabitants full of hookworm and malaria." Instead he found, "a country town full of charm and even beauty." He goes on to register his surprise at the quality of the town's infrastructure and economy:

> The houses are surrounded by pretty gardens, with cool green lawns and stately trees. The two chief streets are paved from curb to curb. The stores carry good stocks and have a metropolitan air, especially the drug, book, magazine, sporting goods and soda-water emporium of the estimable Robinson. A few of the town ancients still affect galluses and string ties, but the younger bucks are very nattily turned out. Scopes himself, even in his shirt sleeves, would fit into any college campus in America save that of Harvard alone.[6]

Soon enough the court proceedings soured Mencken's view of idyllic Dayton. In the end, he considered the rural and small-town people of Dayton stupid for privileging the Bible's account of creation over the theory of evolution. "They know little if anything that is worth knowing," he said, "and there is not the slightest sign of a natural desire among them to increase their knowledge." This is a problem not just in Dayton, he said, but also among the vast majority of Americans who live outside of cities. It's a remarkable observation not only because it is crass and condescending but also because of the sheer scope of his denunciation. At the time he proclaimed the hordes of Americans outside of cities to be woefully ignorant, half of the American population was considered rural and the other half lived mostly in villages and small towns.[7]

Mencken couldn't wait to get out of small-town America. He's not the only one.

There's a strong clear message in American culture that rural and small-town places are for leaving. Maybe there's no shame in being raised there—maybe there is. But when you have a chance to take matters into your own hands, the best thing you can do is leave. It's an idea so dear to us that it has anthems in popular culture. The narrator in Bruce Springsteen's 1975 breakout album *Born to Run* spends forty minutes describing the "town full of losers" he lives in and making plans of "pulling out of here to win."[8] He paints vivid pictures of dead-end jobs and useless high school diplomas and disappointment and addiction in small-town New Jersey that shrinks in shame in the shadow of Manhattan. He articulates America's centuries-old sentiment about small towns when he says, "We gotta get out while we're young."[9]

For many Americans, real opportunity lives outside small-town and rural America. You gotta get out while you're young.

That's what I did. I left Arkansas for Chicagoland. My dad told me growing up, "Find a job you love and you'll never work a day in your life." That lesson took root. None of the jobs I wanted were available to me in Arkansas, at least not without an advanced education that I could only get somewhere else. So days after I got married, my wife and I did what our national mythology says we should do: we packed up our car and left small-town middle America to live near a glittering metropolis.

6

You Never Know What Might Happen to You in the Suburbs

Wheaton, Illinois

Within a month of our wedding, I was hospitalized and hooked up to an IV to treat severe dehydration caused by a particularly ugly case of mono. They call it the kissing disease. For me it resulted in very little kissing during the first few weeks of marriage. Instead, we fulfilled the "in sickness" part of our vows along with the "for poorer" part right at the beginning.

It was a rough start to our life together in Wheaton, Illinois. We arrived in town in the bleak midwinter just in time for me to start graduate school classes in the January term. Amy was looking for work. I was attending class and getting sicker by the day. It took a couple of weeks to diagnose the illness. The weather was frigid. There were no signs of human life on the sidewalks. The days were short. We were sick and cold and poor and lonely.

Our plan was to live in Wheaton long enough for me to

finish my master's degree—three semesters—and then move somewhere else. We were eager to find a church, since we wouldn't be in town long. We had visited a few before I got good and sick. Then we missed a few weeks in a row. When I was well enough to resume the search, we went back to one of the churches we'd visited before. They remembered our names. They told us they missed us the weeks we were gone, and we believed them. The worship wasn't really our style, but we reasoned we would only be around a year and a half.

We stayed nearly a decade.

Soon enough, our entire experience of Wheaton changed. Once the spring thaw came and the days got longer, people poured out of their homes and apartments to soak up the sunlight. Church gave us a community of close friends of a range of ages. We still had no money. But we were happy.

It's tempting (and easy) to hate on the suburbs these days. In popular culture since the 1980s, and increasingly, it seems, in recent years, the suburbs represent the worst part of the American dream. Suburbia—epitomized by cookie-cutter houses, vapid consumerism, and affluent white people—is American capitalism gone to seed. These perceptions persist despite the fact that suburban demographics have shifted so that they are more diverse, both culturally and socioeconomically.[1]

I had never used the term *suburban* to describe a place I'd lived. There was town and country. We didn't have any *–urbs*, so we didn't have any *sub*urbs. Over time I learned the score and realized I was in a new kind of place. Not just a small town with more stuff and not the city just up the road. Chicagoland encompasses almost 11,000 square miles in three states and is home to nearly ten million people. The majority of the region is neither small-town nor urban. It's something altogether different.

I didn't have strong feelings about suburban life, either. Because the suburban landscape struck me as quite a bit like the small towns I'd lived in before—only bigger—I moved there without any preconceptions of "the burbs." The easy access to dining and shopping, the big houses and lawns, were all really attractive to me. My brother-in-law lived in the city and had a lot to say about it. He always complained about driving "out to the suburbs."

"You guys should drive into the city," he'd say. "It's such a long way *out* to the suburbs."

As if the distance were different the other way around.

Maybe it makes us basic white people, but we found life in the suburbs perfectly delightful and almost *entirely* delightful for the eight years we lived there. We made it past the seven-year itch in our marriage and adopted our first child there. We became adults in Wheaton. We suffered and grieved and experienced the greatest Christian community we've experienced, before or since, as a family. Paradoxically it was the first place that made me aware of profound regional differences in America and within the church.

New Way of Engaging Culture

We moved to Wheaton for graduate school, which means that a central part of our experience in the suburbs was interconnected with Christian higher education. I expected the transition to be smooth because I was going to school and I was pretty good at school. It became apparent within the first few class periods that my academic experience here was going to be very different than my experience growing up and very different even than college in Arkansas.

Part of the adjustment had to do with the subject matter itself. I majored in biblical studies and English in college, with a minor in Hebrew. My Baptist college experience was very different from my Baptist church experience growing up. Even so, in both cases, the clear emphasis fell on interpreting the Bible. Nearly all of my academic study before graduate school was primarily biblical studies. We had very little systematic theology and church history. One of the first courses I took in graduate school was a theology course in which, after reading a selection from a Reformation-era theologian, the professor asked: "What is the appropriate Augustinian response to this statement?"

I didn't even understand the question.

He was assuming that any Christian student in a course like this had at least a cursory understanding of Christian history and tradition. Before that time, the terms "Christian history" and "tradition" meant to me whatever my local church did since the 1950s. In other words, the experience of being a Christian student studying Christian subject matter was considerably different.

A significant part of that change included the fact that if you're studying the Bible, the most important source you have to deal with is the Bible. When you start asking questions about theology and culture, the source material changes. You have to read literature and engage the arts. Instead of retreating from secular intellectual sources, you have to engage them. As a child I had avoided a lot of these materials because I was a Christian. Here I was being asked to engage these materials precisely because I was a Christian.

This different orientation toward culture wasn't limited to academia. The Christian suburban population had a very different posture toward culture than what I grew up with. They went to movies. There was wine and beer at every Christian get-together. They took pride in reading good fiction and consuming secular art and music. The instinctive resistance in which I was discipled was replaced here by an instinctive consumption and acceptance. I had entered college with a goal to learn what I needed to learn to *resist* secular intellectualism. Now I was in a world that was preparing students to *engage* secular intellectualism. I didn't have the vocabulary for it, but I was moving from fundamentalism to evangelicalism.

> *I had entered college with a goal to learn what I needed to resist secular intellectualism. Now I was in a world that was preparing students to engage it.*

Over time, I learned the reason for this: not only was the *way* of engaging culture different here, so too was the *goal* of engaging culture.

Early in my first semester, I visited my faculty adviser to talk about what courses I should take. In college I had a double major and a minor, I explained, so I didn't have a lot of space in my schedule for electives. For that reason, I'd never been strategic about what courses I took. I just took what my advisers suggested that I take.

My adviser looked up from the papers on his desk long enough to say, "I guess it's time to grow up."

His "advice" stunned me. I took him to mean that it was time for me to take control of my education and make the hard decisions I needed to make in order to succeed. The thing was, I made it to grad school by myself. My parents and others offered moral support, to be sure. But they'd given no guidance and offered no financial support. I felt like I had accomplished something just by making it this far. Now I was realizing this was only the beginning.

For the first time I felt alien in school. J. D. Vance, author of *Hillbilly Elegy*, described a similar sensation during his first year of law school. "Yale planted a seed of doubt in my mind about whether I belonged," Vance writes. "I lived among newly christened members of what folks back home pejoratively call the 'elites,' and by every outward appearance, I was one of them: I am a tall, white, straight male." While our personal details vary, I resonated deeply with Vance's conclusion: "I have never felt out of place in my entire life. But I did at Yale."[2]

My adviser's comment came to represent for me a general expectation that education *here* was going to work the way education worked at any reputable graduate school. That is, my hometown faith experience operated as if the culture still belonged to Christians, but it was gradually (and systematically) being taken away. Our resistance was important because it helped stem the inevitable onslaught of non-Christian culture.

At Wheaton I learned that many educated Christians

view the situation differently. The culture has already become entirely secularized, and all its institutions—education, government, culture making, and more—operate by a set of agreed-upon rules. The goal of this new kind of Christianity I encountered in the suburbs was to have a seat at the table. More than that, we wanted to demonstrate that we are the intellectual and creative equals of the secular establishment. If we wanted a seat at the table and if we wanted to be taken seriously, we were going to have to accommodate and play by their rules.

I suppose it *was* time to grow up.

This orientation toward culture—engaging and playing by the rules—was an intentional decision. It wasn't simple accommodation. The folks I knew who were engaging in these conversations did so because they thought it was the most effective way of advancing Christian scholarship and art and politics. To be honest, I was beginning to agree. My studies in American Christian history were focused on the differences between fundamentalism and evangelicalism. It took studying the difference to realize that I was raised as a fundamentalist. And the people I now learned from and worked with were actively rejecting the fundamentalist approach to culture— resistance and withdrawal. I believed they were onto something.

The problem, of course, is that by rejecting a fundamentalist approach to culture, we had to reject fundamentalism and fundamentalists altogether. That is, my new Christian community viewed my old Christian community not simply as wrong but also as embarrassing and even damaging to the cause of Christ. Instead of dismissing evolution as a tool of the devil, for example, my new Christian community was willing to accept it, or at least parts of it, as compatible with a theistic worldview in order to engage the broader conversation about creation. Anyone who wasn't willing to do this was part of the problem, not part of the solution.

Again, I generally agreed that the culture wars were over and that we had lost and that a new approach to the most important issues was in order. But breaking with my childhood approach to both my faith and my orientation to the broader American culture was going to cost me a lot. It was going to cost me to sacrifice some of the values shared by my original moral community. It was going to put distance between me and the people who, whatever their faults and failures, brought me up in the faith.

As much as my new community wanted a seat at the table with the broader culture, I felt like my old Christian community was being excluded from the Christian table. I was willing to depart from the things that weren't helpful. But I wasn't willing to abandon my heritage altogether.

As much as my new community wanted a seat at the table with the broader culture, I felt like my old Christian community was being excluded from the Christian table.

Philip Jenkins's book *The Next Christendom* made the startling case in 2002 that the "average" Christian was changing.[3] If in the middle of the twentieth century, the average Christian in the world was white and Western, the average Christian by the mid-twenty-first century will be nonwhite and non-Western. That means too that typical evangelical belief will no longer be determined by what American evangelicals believe and do but by the faith embodied by evangelicals in the Global South (i.e., what is sometimes called the "developing world" or "third world").

What will this new faith and practice look like? Jenkins spelled that out a couple years later in *The New Faces of Christianity*.[4] First of all, Jenkins observed, the new evangelicals are agrarian, which means they have a more intuitive understanding of the Old Testament world and parables of Jesus. They are more communal and collectivistic than Westerners, who tend to be individualistic. Therefore, Global South Christians care about clans and families and the land that belongs to them. Finally, these new global evangelicals have a strong belief in spirits and the spirit world. They therefore take the Bible's language about spiritual warfare, etc., very seriously.

The book spurred (or at least preceded) a ton of books on the views of Christians around the world. As it should. I couldn't help but chafe, though, at what felt like hypocrisy. Rural Christians in America have similar perspectives as those Jenkins describes. One Sunday morning in my first pastorate, I showed up to church only to discover that all the men were missing. It was just me and the women. One of the women explained that the men were all in the fields working because the hay had been cut earlier that week and there was rain in the forecast for today. Rain ruins cut hay. So the men were working their way from farm to farm, baling and hauling hay to keep it from spoiling in the rain. Not all rural people are farmers, but they nevertheless lived closer to the land than the average suburbanite or city dweller. Rural Americans are more collectivistic than the general population, which is why they are often suspicious of outsiders. They have a corporate identity to protect, not just an individual identity. And most of the Christians I grew up with not only took the Bible seriously; they took it *literally*.

Why, I wondered, are evangelical scholars not interested, too, in rural American readings of the Scriptures? An important part of the answer to that question, of course, is that many suburban Christian scholars are embarrassed by rural and small-town Christians. Instead of being celebrated, the qualities rural Americans share with the Global South are denigrated in rural Americans. Their agrarian perspective is often perceived as backward; their collectivistic identity is viewed as xenophobic; their sensitivity to the spiritual realm is superstitious.

It began to strike me as a bit insincere to hear evangelical scholars lament that our faith tradition had borrowed too freely from the Enlightenment and that our faith had been co-opted by modernistic habits of mind, only to turn around and denounce rural Americans as fundamentalists whose views of Scripture and the life of faith were outdated and outmoded. The idea that the rural church might be an intellectual resource didn't seem to enter anyone's mind. There was, it seemed to me, a clear bias against a rural and small-town way of being Christian.

Looking back, I guess what was happening in grad school is that I was beginning (just beginning) to recognize the limits of my own point of view. At the same time, I wanted my point of view to be considered and valued without amendment.

What made the whole process more difficult and more uncomfortable was that at the same time that I was being challenged academically to distance myself from the kind of Christianity I grew up with, I was also becoming self-conscious about my regional background.

Rural Southerners, myself included, have been, and frequently are, stereotyped and made fun of, not only about major issues such as racism and misogyny but also for small things like how we talk, dress, eat, and relax. So I learned to neutralize my Southern accent to avoid the same old conversations about Arkansas—

"You're from Arkansas?"

"I didn't know they wore shoes there!"

"And you can *read*. Well done!"

"Do you play the banjo?"

A lot of those comments were made by people who came from similar places. They were proud to have left. I was undecided.

I never thought of myself as rural, really, until I moved to the suburban Midwest, and I was gently teased or openly disparaged. That is, I didn't identify myself with particular values until those values were under attack. My sense is that a lot of people do this. I have family members who have never in my life cared about owning a gun until a liberal Democrat became president. In that moment they became much more concerned about the Second Amendment than they had ever been before. We make minor things into major things when we feel attacked. That happens on a regional scale all the time.

I was being acculturated into a new community with different sensibilities. In my academic and professional life, it was an uncomfortable transformation. Church provided a safe place for a similar sort of transformation to take place.

A Thick Network of Friendships

The popular image of the suburbs as superficially friendly but profoundly isolated—with everyone retreating to their high-fenced backyard instead of socializing with the neighbors—may match the experience of some people. But that isn't how my wife and I experienced it. We experienced open doors and intentional neighborliness and unfussy hospitality.

Because we were all in town for graduate school, we were in relationship with several married couples all in roughly the same stage of life. Being all about equally broke, we found cheap ways to have a good time. On summer Sundays after church, we took our leftovers and random cuts of meat to someone's apartment complex to grill. For nearly every long weekend and Hallmark holiday, we gathered to eat and play games, watch movies, and enjoy free concerts in the park. With one couple we had a standing Monday evening date to watch a favorite TV show. One week we would meet at their place and they cooked; the next week we would meet at our place and we cooked.

In addition to casual gatherings, we had something like a formal rhythm of fellowship. The wife in one couple was from New Orleans, and she hosted a Mardi Gras party every year that included gumbo and king cake shipped north from New

Orleans. Other friends hosted a chili dinner every fall, and we (the O'Briens) claimed St. Patrick's Day. Others hosted Memorial Day and Fourth of July and more. We spent holidays with one another and got together when someone's parents came to town. We were a little family of expats from around the country making the most of graduate school life in the suburbs.

No doubt part of what made for good community is that we were young and, for most of our time in town, childless. But our relationships weren't limited to people our age. We also had a thick network of friendships with people who were older than we were and could help us navigate adulthood. This community became especially valuable for us in hard times. We walked the hard road of infertility in the suburbs and were embraced by a church family that sustained us and endured our pain with us.

Every other Tuesday morning I met with a group of men from church at six in the morning before we all headed off to work, some of them into the city. Most mornings we just ate and laughed together. Often someone shared devotional thoughts. The lasting gift they gave me was wisdom and patience.

There were missteps, to be sure. Even great community comes with undesirable side effects. One Wednesday evening during Lent, I shared a testimony of God's faithfulness during our struggle to get pregnant. It was the first time we were sharing the news with anyone other than close friends or family. The congregation was immediately supportive. Someone told us, "It took us several years to get pregnant with our first. We never learned why. Those were very difficult times. We're very sorry."

Another woman asked my wife, in front of me, "Is it possible that you are allergic to his sperm?"

I didn't know that was possible. The bigger issue, of course, was I couldn't believe she said "sperm" in church. But there we were.

Our struggle to become pregnant became, over time, a decision to adopt. More than once we had close calls, near placements that fell through. Our Christian community, old and young, gave generously in all ways and walked us through it. Friends paid for counseling and cooked us meals. When our oldest son came home somewhat suddenly, they waited around in the aisles at Target until we completed a gift registry. They laughed with us and wept with us.

Some would have you believe it's impossible to form so many good, rich memories at chain restaurants and in cookie-cutter suburban houses.

Growing in New Directions

Our communities, both the academic and church communities, changed us. A more engaged approach to culture meant appreciating the arts and wrestling with hard ideas posed by thinkers. That suited me. Even though the world we lived in was ethnically homogenous, it was much more diverse in other ways. Theologically—well, we were now living where all those Lutherans lived before they retired to my hometown. Politically, I loved that during election seasons we saw bumper stickers for candidates from *all* parties in our church parking lot. Some members drank alcohol. Some abstained.

The boundary markers between in and out were drawn in more pleasant places.

After graduate school I started my career in Christian publishing. The way our community and education changed us prepared me to enter this new field. That new field, I soon learned, shared the sensibilities of my new suburban Christian community. Publishers were open to the culture and to science and to business. They were willing to critique those things, and that meant they had to engage them, and to engage them they had to have a certain level of fluency. Where the watchword of my childhood faith was "resist," the new watchword was "engage."

And this personal and professional growth had consequences, both good ones and hard ones.

In the time we lived in Wheaton, I earned a master's degree and a PhD. I worked in Christian publishing as a writer and editor. I was moving deeper into the evangelical establishment and culturally moving further from my childhood experience of faith and life. My orientation and posture toward culture and church and other Christians were changing. Applying for teaching jobs around the country, I realized that the ways I was growing were preparing me to belong in a wide range of places similar to the Chicago suburbs—Grand Rapids, Minneapolis, Orange County.

If I'm honest, while I was becoming better suited for professional suburban culture, I feared I was becoming less imaginable to my family all the time. As a response, I tried to recover and embrace parts of my childhood I felt slipping away or maligned. I started making trips home to Arkansas for guy time with my dad, where I transgressed by enjoying things that would have made my cultured suburban friends uncomfortable—things like shooting guns.

On one trip to Arkansas for a guys' weekend, my dad led me to a still pond in the woods where he thought we might have luck catching fish. The water was dark and covered in algae like the lake water I spent so much time in and on as a child. For the first time in my life, I thought the water seemed dirty. Whatever creatures might be in there didn't worry me. But imagine the germs!

Dad waded right in. I hesitated but tried to play it cool.

After a few minutes my dad voiced his relief that I waded in with him. "It's good to see you doing the things you grew up doing," he said. "Honestly, I was a little afraid you'd gotten citified."

The idea that I no longer fit in among the people who raised me stung as much as the implication that I didn't belong where I lived in the suburbs, attending a prestigious Christian graduate school. And yet there was truth in it. To fit in with the community in which I was working so hard to succeed, I had to develop fluency in a new tongue. Whatever I did for a living in the evangelical establishment, whether it was teaching at a college or seminary, working for a publisher, or serving a nonprofit, odds were I would be living and working in the suburbs. That's where most of those organizations seemed to be. I was beginning to fit in there.

A reviewer said of my first published article that I was clearly an "educated elitist out of touch with the middle class." The charge was so laughable that I've memorized it. I was in my early 20s and broke. Economically, I was clawing my way up to the middle class. Culturally, I hailed from people who shoot guns indoors. I found the critique so ridiculous that I've always wanted to have it ironed on a T-shirt or, perhaps a better homage to my upbringing, cross-stitched on a throw pillow.

And yet—

It's true that I was changing.

All my life my dad had told me, "Find a job you love and you'll never work a day in your life." The jobs I wanted were in the suburbs, and I was learning to thrive there. Kathleen Norris describes this situation in *Dakota*, a book of reflections on rural life on the plains. There, she says:

> Parents must raise their children for the world outside; there are few job opportunities here. And the young are both rewarded and punished for defecting: proud parents make sure that the local paper prints stories about their children's activities in college, but on returning home for the summer, these students often find they've become outsiders on their home ground.[5]

In some ways that felt like growth. In some ways it felt like a betrayal. Becoming fitter for the establishment made me less fit for my hometown and our way of life.

My wife experienced our entire time in Wheaton differently than I did. The Americans she grew up with as an expat in Singapore were from places like Wheaton. She longed for greater diversity in our community the whole time we were there. I longed for a deeper sense of validation of my childhood experiences and the communities that formed me.

In retrospect, I recognize signs that there were other people, too, who did not experience the suburbs the way I did. For a couple of summers I worked with a special events company that set up and tore down for major events in the city of Chicago. One night we had a job in the suburbs, not far from where I lived. I was thrilled because it meant a short commute. Other members of our crew were less thrilled. At the end of the job, in the wee hours of the morning, one of our guys, a young African American man, started walking back to his car. Before he could get too far, an older African American man on the crew shouted after him.

"Wait up," he said. "I don't want you walking to your car alone. You never know what might happen to you in the suburbs."

Learning to Tell the Whole Truth

"The problem with stereotypes is not that they are untrue, but that they are incomplete. They make one story become the only story."

—Chimamanda Adichie[1]

When novelist Chimamanda Adichie moved to the United States from Nigeria for college, she encountered for the first time an American perception of Africans. Adichie's roommate was shocked she spoke English, shocked she knew how to use modern appliances, shocked they shared a taste in music: Mariah Carey.

The roommate's surprise caught Adichie off guard. She grew up in a middle-class Nigerian family, the daughter of a college professor and administrator. The family employed live-in domestic help. She learned English from childhood, because English is Nigeria's national language. The two probably had quite a bit in common. "What struck me," Adichie says of her roommate's expectations, "was this":

She had felt sorry for me even before she saw me. Her default position toward me, as an African, was a kind of patronizing, well-meaning pity. My roommate had a single story of Africa: a single story of catastrophe. In this single story, there was no possibility of Africans being similar to her in any way, no possibility of feelings more complex than pity, no possibility of a connection as human equals.[2]

The question, of course, is why? Why was it possible for the reality of Adichie's childhood experience and her American roommate's expectations to be so dramatically different? Adichie proposes that the problem lies in the "single story" Americans hear about Africa. The vast majority of Americans do not know Africa by experience. They only know about the continent through media—the news or movies or even the accounts of missions agencies and aid organizations. These media outlets, as different as they might be, typically communicate a consistent message about Africa and Africans to American audiences. Adichie explains that after a few years in the US, the source of her roommate's surprise became clear.

If I had not grown up in Nigeria, and if all I knew about Africa were from popular images, I too would think that Africa was a place of beautiful landscapes, beautiful animals, and incomprehensible people, fighting senseless wars, dying of poverty and AIDS, unable to speak for themselves and waiting to be saved by a kind, white foreigner.[3]

The "single story" reduces all the complexity of a place or people group into a single-dimensional image that may capture some small part of the picture but, over time, begins to stand in for the *whole* picture. The way to create a single story, Adichie explains, is to "show a people as one thing, as *only* one thing, over and over again, and that is what they become." The dangerous refugee, for example, or the homophobic evangelical. Adichie admits that not only has she experienced being reduced by the single story, she has also "bought into the single story." During a trip to Mexico she discovered "that I had been so immersed in the media coverage of Mexicans that they had become one thing in my mind, the abject immigrant."[4]

> *The "single story" reduces all the complexity of a place or people group into a single-dimensional image that, over time, begins to stand in for the whole picture.*

It is tempting to believe the single story because it is easy. It is dangerous to believe the single story because it is *too* easy.

Geography and the Single Story

The idea of the single story is a great way to diagnose why Americans from different regions of the country and different types of communities—urban, rural, suburban, and such—feel they know what those places are like even if they've never been there. The single story helps explain the strong emotional reaction people all across America, including Christians, have about places with which they have very little personal experience. Popular culture repeats and reinforces certain narratives and stereotypes about every type of community. I would be willing to bet that most people eventually and unconsciously adopt one of these narratives as their single story of each of these places.

Consider these common narratives about each of the types of communities below. For the sake of discussion, I've chosen two each:

Rural and Small Town

Rural and small-town America is home to backward simpletons who may be kind and moral but are intellectually inferior.

Rural and small-town America is home to patriarchal, misogynistic, homophobic, and xenophobic moralists who use religion to mask dangerous and outdated values.

Suburbs

The suburbs are home to affluent (and primarily white) professionals and their families, who have chosen to sacrifice adventure for security.

The placid façade of the suburbs masks profound evil and dysfunction, hidden away behind picket fences or in secret finished basements.

Cities

Cities are glittering lands of opportunity that attract the most accomplished talent and become the gathering ground for cultural elites.

Cities are festering pits of crime and human deviance.

Each of these narratives persists because there is some evidence to support them. Stereotypes always exist for a reason. But, as Adichie describes it, "The problem with stereotypes is not that they are untrue, but that they are incomplete. They make *one* story become the *only* story"[5] (emphasis mine). And they can only survive by reducing and extracting the single story out of the multidimensional reality. Over the last decade, for example, I have noted the selective plundering of what others felt could be salvaged from our rural roots—crafting, canning, gardening, and the popularity of folk music. These things have been extracted from rural identity and all that is left in the popular imagination is the single story: "They get bitter, they cling to guns or religion or antipathy to people who aren't like them or anti-immigrant sentiment or anti-trade sentiment as a way to explain their frustrations."[6]

The power of the single story helps explain a dynamic I have witnessed time and again. I know people who distrust a people group—say, an ethnic group or "city folk"—as a *group* but who nevertheless respect and enjoy the company of an *individual* from that group with whom they work:

People, for example, who complain about "the blacks" but are good neighbors to their African American colleague.

People who hate or fear rural America but embrace me, for example, as safe and sane.

Friends who hate Christianity but keep inviting us Christians to parties.

In every case, the person has bought into a single story about the group. And because they recognize that an individual that they actually know doesn't fit the single story, they view the person as an exception to the single story rather than allowing their experience with that person to *alter* the single story. Their experience with the individual isn't enough to change their perception of the group. Instead, the single story survives even direct experiences that challenge or undermine it.

The truth is, it takes lots of exposure to lots of people who don't fit the story before most of us would consider discarding the story or revising it in favor of something more complex. It takes exception after exception after exception before we realize these individuals aren't exceptions after all. They are the *rule*. Developing that level of familiarity with enough people who are different from you is hard and awkward and challenging. It doesn't happen by accident. It requires intentionality. It requires humility. It requires repentance.

> *Developing that level of familiarity with enough people who are different from you is challenging. It requires intentionality, humility, and repentance.*

A colleague of mine exemplifies these qualities, and he has allowed them to change his single story about white America. An ethnic minority who has only lived in cities, he recently saw the movie *I, Tonya*, which is a fictionalized, documentary style account of the 1994 incident in which figure skater Nancy Kerrigan was attacked by an assailant after she left the ice during a training session. Fellow skater Tonya Harding was implicated in the attack. *I, Tonya* tells the story from Harding's perspective.

The film focuses on Harding's difficult childhood in a lower-class family ruled by a demanding and un-nurturing mother. The dynamics of poverty and domestic violence and classism in Harding's white American life are portrayed movingly in the film. And they were news to my colleague.

"I didn't know there were white people who lived like that," he told me after he watched the movie. "As soon as I finished it, I made my kids watch it, too. They need to see that."

Many in my friend's position would likely have seen Harding's story as an exception to the single story of the white experience in America. My friend took the story to heart and decided that there must be others like Harding out there. Maybe he didn't have a full picture of what life is like for some people in other parts of the country or even in his own city.

Good Stewards of Stories

As Adichie said in a 2009 TEDGlobal presentation:[7] In the age of twenty-four-hour news and polarized national politics, humility has very little advantage. The advantage comes from holding the power to decide the single stories. That is why we have equal and opposite media sources, liberal and conservative, both with the goal of convincing their constituents of the truth of their narrative as they tell it. We claw at each other's faces and gnaw on each other's backs for the power to tell the story. These things don't just "happen." We create them. And they have consequences.

This struggle for the power to tell the story has spiritual consequences. Take as an example the single story that rural places are for leaving, because the real opportunities lie in other places. Wendell Berry spoke about the spiritual consequences of the single story for rural communities in a profound reflection on "the practice . . . of using the rural ministry as a training ground for young ministers and as a means of subsidizing their education." Berry has in mind a practice in which I participated: learning in ministry by serving in small, country churches.[8] This was what I was encouraged to do. My spiritual mentors suggested it. Cut your teeth in a small country church, make your mistakes and gain confidence, so you can be better prepared for a *real* job in ministry after college. Young pastors rarely stay in these churches. They remain until they've earned their credentials and done their time.

Berry concludes from this that the "denominational hierarchies, then, evidently regard country places in exactly the same way as 'the economy' does: as sources of economic power to be exploited for the advantage of 'better' places. The country people will be used to educate ministers for the benefit of city people (in wealthier churches) who, obviously, are thought more deserving of educated ministers." Practices like this send a clear message to the congregations involved, and the "message that country people get from their churches, then, is the same message that they get from 'the economy':

that, as country people, they do not matter much and do not deserve much consideration."[9]

Our commitment to the single story, to simple stereotypes, has consequences. It affects everything from how we vote to how we prepare candidates for vocational ministry. It affects how we engage new places.

I moved from Arkansas to America's most densely populated city carrying my own single story about the place. I was as surprised as anyone to discover the truth.

8

A New York State of Mind

Manhattan

On the day we moved to New York, we took off from an airport with only one terminal and one runway in my hometown of Bentonville, Arkansas. The airport is surrounded by farmland dotted with cows and round hay bales. The drive to the airport winds through hollers and over creeks I explored as a child. I pointed out to our kids as we drove, "Daddy used to fish there with his friends," or "That's where Daddy and his friend went camping once, just the two of us, when we were very young."

Construction on the airport began when I was in high school and, under the policy of eminent domain, displaced a number of families from our church whose houses were torn down to make room for the runway. I learned to despise the project as evidence of government overreach or corporate greed, or possibly both. Recently I learned that the sale of family farms, while a sentimental loss, made some locals millionaires overnight. Even so, the airport had opened twenty years earlier, and I'd never been inside. It was odd to be flying out of an airport that my family once opposed.

We landed at LaGuardia a few hours later after a long final descent that circled Manhattan. Out our left-hand window we saw the Statue of Liberty, the Brooklyn Bridge, the Chrysler Building, and a number of other landmarks we'd shown our kids in the children's book we bought to help them adjust to the idea of their new home.

All our furniture and other worldly belongings had been shipped with movers weeks before—or so we hoped—and unloaded into our new apartment. It occurred to me as we wheeled our luggage to the taxi stand that no one knew us in our new building. No one had ever seen us before. I'd only been there once, for a few minutes, just long enough to tell the rental agent, "We'll take it." Someone could have burgled us at a leisurely pace over the last two weeks before we arrived. I knew it was possible to break into the apartment. My real estate agent did it when we visited.

"Hold my purse," she said. Then she opened the apartment door with a credit card.

It was the second apartment she broke into that morning. The other had already been rented and, much to the surprise of everyone involved, was inhabited at the time. More than a year later I told a realtor friend in New York that our agent had broken into our apartment on preview day.

"That's a good agent," he said matter-of-factly. I suppose she was.

The weight of our decision to move settled as we drove

through Queens, then turned north along the Harlem River to head uptown to our new neighborhood. These places were almost mythical to us, known to us only through books or television shows or movies. I knew from reading *The Cross and the Switchblade* that a street gang stabbed a boy some nineteen times outside Highbridge Pool, just a couple blocks east of our new apartment, back in 1958. I knew that stabbing attracted a country preacher named David Wilkerson to the city to minister to street kids. I knew some of the kids had lived in Spanish Harlem, which we could see now out our car windows. My impression of Times Square was from the movie *Big* and others like it, which gave me visions of neon strip club signs and peep show ads. What I knew of the Upper West Side I knew from movies like *You've Got Mail*, with its boutique cafés and bookshops. All to say, we were moving to a city that most Americans feel they know but that most know only from a distorting distance. I knew already from short visits here—and from long years in suburban Chicago—that other people's assumptions about the rural South were frequently wrong. I was beginning to wonder how much I really knew about the city as we hurried down narrow streets between tall buildings and experienced the disorienting verticality of Manhattan firsthand.

Because it was easier and cheaper for me to travel alone, I had made a trip to New York myself a few weeks before to hunt for an apartment. It cost a fortune to move in. With broker fees and deposit and first month's rent, the total came to more than our mortgage for an entire year in Arkansas. Neither my wife nor my children had ever seen the place I rented. They hadn't even seen the neighborhood. Today, when we all moved in together, they would all see our new home for the first time.

When we arrived at the building, the foyer seemed older and dirtier than I remembered it. Developers built scores of buildings like ours in Washington Heights in the 1930s as affordable housing for city workers, six-story buildings that retained their Gilded-Age charm but were also evidence of their age. The superintendent gave us the keys, and we headed up to the third floor. Much to my relief, the apartment was full of boxes and furniture. Everything appeared to be accounted for. We set my son up at a desk to build a Lego set and my daughter drawing so we could unpack. We opened the windows and were grateful for the cool breeze, the urban soundtrack of light traffic, Latin music, and the occasional siren.

We made it.

Later my wife and I were putting dishes away in the kitchen cabinet in our new eighteen-square-foot kitchen.

"It's really lovely," she said.

"It is, isn't it," I said. "I'm so glad you like it."

"We're going to be happy here."

We looked out the kitchen window, out over the street, where a full, green tree cast shadows on the brownstone across the street. It grew there in lovely defiance of the hardscape of concrete and steel and brick that surrounded it. Its leaves fluttered softly in the early summer breeze.

A man stumbled up the sidewalk and stopped square in front of our window. He threw up on the sidewalk, wiped his mouth, and wandered on.

I've shared this story with several of our new friends from Manhattan. They typically respond the same way:

"Welcome to New York."

A Different Way of
Sticking Yourself into the World

Right up until we left for New York City, folks with good intentions warned us about the dangers of city life and urged us to be careful. They wanted us to assume a defensive posture before we even arrived, like the character Bonnie in David Sedaris's story "City of Angels," who lands at Kennedy Airport "convinced that, given half a chance, the people of New York would steal the fillings right out of her mouth."[1]

We weren't afraid, but we did want to adjust to and fit in with our new home as soon as possible, even if our motivations were different. My primary motivation was fear of scorn. Every time I spoke, I feared what people heard was, "Well, I'll be dadgummed. Them buildings sure is tall." I wanted to pass for a local as soon as possible for fear that my rural roots might embarrass me.

My wife had a different motivation. Having grown up as an American expatriate in Singapore, Amy identifies as a "third culture kid." She is American by nationality but spent all her formative years in Asia. She's tall and blond and has green eyes—clearly not Asian. But she *feels* Asian in important ways. So she was always perceived as an outsider in her home in Singapore. When she moved to the States, she was perceived as an American but *felt* like a newcomer.

From neither here nor there, she's from some other place, a "third" culture. For this reason, learning the cultural rules and adopting them quickly so as to belong is important for her. As quickly as possible, she wanted to pass as *from* New York.

The goal of fitting in quickly might have been easier to achieve if we had moved without children. But we did not. One of our children cooperated with Project Assimilation, but overall our profound desire to appear local was stymied by our children who made us conspicuous from the beginning. We gave ourselves away as newcomers when we nearly were separated from our son on the subway platform. And for most of that first summer, our daughter's profound aversion to the subway in general made us stand out as newbies more thoroughly than if we'd been wearing hats that said, "WE'RE NEW."

Early on, our daughter developed a particularly effective form of protest against the subway: she went limp. On one trip home from the grocery store, she went limp and spread-eagle on her back in protest between the automatic doors as we were leaving, a silent but clear pronouncement of her displeasure to be headed back to the subway. With grocery bags in both hands, I eventually coaxed her to her feet (with both kind encouragement and whispered threats), and we made it a few yards before she went limp again—facedown—this time in the crosswalk. A few minutes later she fell prostrate on the filthy subway stairs. Then again on the subway platform. Then again on the floor of the subway itself. It took us nearly an hour to travel two blocks from the store to the train.

If there's an upside to all of this, it's that our daughter now has both an extraordinary immune system and the dubious distinction of having thrown one of her fits in front of an Emmy-nominated star of a hit television show on the Upper West Side. I like to think he talks about her lie-in at fancy parties.

All this is to say that instead of warning us about the *people* of New York, we would have been better served if people had warned us about the *place itself*, the way the city imposes very different conditions for all human interactions.

We moved to New York City from Conway, Arkansas, a growing and energetic town northwest of the state's capital city of Little Rock. Conway is home to 65,000 residents who live in a land area of about forty-six square miles. We now live in Manhattan, way up north in the neighborhood of Washington Heights. The island of Manhattan has *half* the land area of Conway—around twenty-three square miles—and is home to almost 1.7 million people. During business hours, when people from surrounding boroughs and states, even, commute into Manhattan for work, the population swells to nearly four million. Between 9 a.m. and 6 p.m., there are more than 170,000 people *per square mile* on the island of Manhattan. That means New York City crams more people into less space than any place I've ever lived. More people use the subway station near our apartment than lived in my home-town when I was a child. There are more people in my *building* than in the town my dad lives in. There are more people in Manhattan during business hours than live in the entire state of Arkansas.

When you put all those people in a small space, such as cramming them into tubes and shooting them through the earth in the morning and evening or housing them on top of each other in tight quarters separated by thin walls, it changes all the rules of engagement. The best we can do is be sensitive to the fact that—as the mildly neurotic narrator of Walker Percy's *The Moviegoer* put it—"people have a different way of sticking themselves into the world"[2] in different places. All we could do is become comfortable with the fact that our adjustment had to happen publicly. We were on display, in all our failures, before massive crowds on sidewalks and subways and in parks and playgrounds.

During our first summer, our primary means of engaging the city and learning its values was through its most public and democratic spaces: subways and parks. It turns out these public spaces, like my summers with grandparents, provide a concentrated dose of urban cultural values. Some days it feels like a near lethal dose. But before you can appreciate the values on display on the subway, you have to understand how the subway *feels*.

For fun, this experience can easily be simulated:

Turn on the shower as hot as the water will get. Let it run until the bathroom is full of steam and the air is humid. If your bathroom vent is quiet and effective, do not turn it on, as this will spoil the effect. If, however, the vent makes a terrible sound and does not remove the damp air, by all means turn it on. Next, invite ten to twelve strangers into the bathroom. Forbid them from talking to or looking at each other. Tell them the door will open in four minutes. Open the door in eight minutes. When the door opens, allow one person to exit and three to enter. Make sure the people who leave are furthest from the door—maybe standing in the bathtub and carrying a rolling suitcase. Encourage the people leaving and entering to pass through the door simultaneously. Every few minutes, turn the hot shower back on. (But people are standing in the shower, you say. That's life.)

Invite someone to play the trumpet.

The subway is both public and private space. It is *public* transportation, but riders do their darnedest to maintain their *private* space, especially during the morning commute. The profound lack of human interaction on the subway was difficult for me to manage at the beginning. As an introvert, I don't mind it at all when other people ignore me. Nevertheless my rural (and especially Southern) rearing leaves me feeling morally obligated to engage even strangers in conversation.

"Lovely weather, isn't it?" or "This heat is terrible, isn't it?" Or, "What beautiful kids you have! Let me show you pictures of mine!"

Soon enough you realize that subway riders during the morning rush are enjoying their final fleeting minutes of solitude before the day begins—albeit in the presence of two hundred strangers. Folks do what folks in small towns might do in their car on the way to work. Women put on makeup. Men fix their hair. People tune each other out to carve out a few inches of privacy; and your co-commuters tune you out to allow you the privacy. Staring is impolite. We're all here at the same time. But we're not here together.

There are, of course, frequent violations of protocol. The soundtrack of my commute one morning was provided by a man across the aisle who sang aloud with his iPhone playlist on an otherwise silent subway car. It was an eclectic playlist—Kansas, Creed, Elton John—and he covered it fairly well until the key change in "Candle in the Wind."

Of course the best of people can be on display on the subway, too, when children are involved. Our youngest was still in a stroller most of the time that first summer in the city, and my wife frequently had to take both kids out by herself. There are very few elevators on the subway system, so taking kids in strollers means lugging the stroller up and down many flights of stairs. Almost without exception, every time she was out alone, someone would help her carry the stroller. The help was often unceremonious—they rarely *ask* if they could help and they rarely wait around for thanks. They just grab the front of the stroller until you're all down the stairs and then set it down and go on their way.

The public-private space of the subway extends up onto the street, at least during the weekday commute.

The insider scoop on sidewalk conduct is this: in walking cities (like New York), the sidewalk is our freeway. It's how people get to work. And just like people in driving cities are antsy behind the wheel in their mad dash to get the kids to school and arrive to work on time, pedestrians in walking cities feel the same way. The reason people seem rude on the sidewalk on a Monday morning, for example, is because they're commuting. Stepping in front of a fast walker, or weaving around on the sidewalk, or slowing down for no reason is like cutting off another car on the interstate. That might earn you a honk and the finger on the highway. It's likely to earn you a shout and the finger on the sidewalk. It is this sidewalk conduct that no doubt earns New Yorkers a reputation for rudeness among tourists. Commuting in New York makes you turn people into obstacles like the pixelated cars in the arcade game Frogger.

For all these reasons, a busy sidewalk can create tense interactions. One morning after I dropped off my son at school, I headed back to the subway station to catch a train further downtown to work. Some accident had delayed service. The platform was hot and still and so full of people that when the next train *finally* pulled in only half of us waiting could even *fit* on the cars.

It's hot underground (I hate sweating).

I was standing shoulder to shoulder with strangers (I'm not crazy about strangers).

My mood was deteriorating. So I decided to walk.

By now I was annoyed and angry and sweating profusely in my work clothes. I was prepared to walk the more than thirty blocks—two miles—to work if that meant I could avoid interacting with another human person.

Somewhere south of 72nd Street, on the west side of Central Park West, I was walking briskly and fuming about my commute. A quiet honk behind me startled me from my self-pity. I turned, annoyed, to discover the honk came from a golf cart driven by a city sanitation worker. In my sweating, cranky mind he was telling me to get out of the way.

I lost it.

There was no one else on the sidewalk. He had plenty of room to pass me without making me move.

"What's wrong with you?" I said. With sweeping, exaggerated motions—like a magician setting up an illusion—I motioned to the wide, empty sidewalk. "There's plenty of room. And you want me to move out of your way?"

Bad moods are contagious. When I went off, he went off. He sped past me in his cart, mumbling and cussing. I heard him say, "I was just trying to not kill you. Maybe I'll just run you over next time."

In my self-pity I had interpreted his gesture of kindness as an act of aggression. This truth hit me within seconds of my behaving like an idiot.

By the time I reached him, he was down the street picking up trash with a long clawed pole. I stopped him and said, "Excuse me."

He acknowledged me. His eyes were combat ready.

"I apologize for the attitude," I said.

His eyes got big. "*Your* attitude!" He said. "I was just trying to let you know I was there, to be nice, to—"

I raised my hands in surrender. "I know, I know. I understand that now. I'm trying to apologize. I was wrong," I said. "I'm sorry."

This time he laughed. His posture changed, softened. He turned his face and shoulders toward me for the first time in our conversation. "It's OK," he said. "I apologize for *my* attitude." He was shaking his head. "Have a good day."

Kindness and anger are both possible in these densely packed areas where people are making their way places in a hurry. That means we experience moments of profound humanity and grace with complete strangers on the sidewalk. This is especially true on the weekends. One Sunday morning as we were walking to church, a woman hurried up to my wife and said, "You're the first woman I've seen this morning. Can you zip me?"

She turned her bare back to Amy, dress unzipped to her hips.

Amy said, "Sure," and zipped her up.

Then off she went.

An Almost Imaginable Childhood

Manhattan is full of green spaces—playgrounds, parks, zoos, sand, and sprinklers. Nearly 14 percent of New York's land area is parks.[3] Taking my children to these places is the best I can do to replicate for my kids the outdoor freedom of my childhood. Just two blocks north of our apartment is a nearly seven-acre park. The kids love to play on the playground equipment, ride their bikes around the trail, and climb the rock outcroppings. We have to warn them to be careful of broken glass and bottle caps—and not to play too close to sleeping indigents. But otherwise the space gives them room to roam, get grit under their fingernails.

When I was their age, or not much older, my parents turned me loose outdoors and told me to be home by mealtime. But there is no consensus in the city about how supervised children ought to be. The full range of parenting styles is on display at the playground. Under the equipment are the helicopter parents, constantly engaging their children in conversation and ready, it seems, to catch them before they hit the ground should they fall from the monkey bars. Twenty or thirty feet away is the next ring of attentive parents, standing alone or clustered in small groups talking, letting their children play alone but ready to intervene if necessary. Further away still, seated on the benches at the playground's perimeter, are the parents reading books or on their phones, letting their kids sort things out on their own. There is, as you can imagine, some tension between these groups of parents. We are torn between wanting to give our children freedom, on the one hand, and wanting to ensure the parents around us know that we're doing our jobs and watching our kids. As one mother put it, "I don't know if I'm afraid for my kids, or if I'm afraid other people will be afraid and will judge me for my lack of fear."[4]

This gets at an important difference between my own rural childhood and my children's urban childhood. For me, work and play were primarily solitary activities. Because we weren't constantly under the watchful eye of strangers, we were free to drive cars underage and to learn to shoot guns and whittle with knives and fish with hooks because there weren't many other people around whose safety we should consider. As much as we enjoyed playing cards and sharing meals with friends and family, we were able to choose when and where and how long to engage with people socially. In the city, our entire life is social—like it or not. The commute, our time at the park, everything is done in public with the eyes of strangers upon us.

What that means practically is that while I spent a lot of my childhood learning how to do tasks like fish and work and cook, my children spend most of their childhood time (right now) learning social skills. Not long ago my son said it was easier making friends in Arkansas than in New York.

"Why?" I asked.

"Because everyone in Arkansas speaks the same language."

He's navigating social realities that are new to me.

It would be wrong to conclude from this that all New Yorkers prefer the more structured childhood their children experience. Some in the city feel the need to give their children more of the kinds of experiences that are natural in rural places. A park called play:groundNYC is an "adventure playground" where children play without parental supervision and have access to materials they can use to build and create. An article describes it this way:

So, what can you expect on a visit to The Yard? Zero interaction from parents. Once you've signed a waiver, you'll be asked to wait outside, while your kids frolic in the 50,000-square-foot free-play space. They'll find loads of recycled materials to craft and create with, including heavy-duty hands-on tools like hammers and saws. Trained "playworkers" are on-site to make sure everyone stays safe.[5]

(I appreciate the effort. But I'm not sure I trust a stranger's kid to play near mine with hammers and saws.)

The truth is, we spend more time outdoors now than we did when we lived in Arkansas. It's just harder. And on a different scale. E. B. White wrote in the twentieth century, "The city is the place for people who like life in tablet form, concentrated: a forest resolved into a single tree, a lake distilled into a fountain, and all the birds of the air embodied in one transient thrush in a small garden."[6]

One day we made a trip to row a boat in Central Park—to have the water experience that was important in my childhood. We rowed a boat and afterward spread out a blanket by the shore to enjoy a picnic together. Just a few minutes into lunch, there was a clap of thunder and then a downpour of biblical scale. My southern folks might call it a "toad strangler" or a "gully washer." The rains came down and the floods came up. There we were, in the middle of one of America's largest urban parks with no transportation, enjoying the great outdoors with no way to escape it. Because we didn't know where the nearest subway entrances were, it took us more than an hour—in the pouring rain—to get home.

I spent my summers learning to drive and being catechized in family stories about our shared ancestry. My children spent their first summer in New York learning to navigate public transportation and figuring out how to engage socially in a diverse neighborhood. These activities require considerably different skills. But the longer we're here, the more I think the values that lie beneath them are more similar than they first appear.

Some of our neighbors have lived in this neighborhood for generations. Their connection to it is as strong as my connection to Lake Bistineau. That connection has been re-inforced through stories about past relations, stories told by generations of men over dominoes in the park. It may not be "sitting till bedtime," but the principle is the same.

On an especially hot Sunday evening in early fall, I walked to the corner bodega for a few groceries and went the long way around. Over the tops of parked cars, I saw the heads of about a dozen young men congregated on the sidewalk—nothing surprising there. What was surprising is that they were all facing the same way: toward the wall and sitting quite still. As I approached I saw they were watching a football game on a large flat screen TV. The cable cord ran in through the window, and the television sat on a TV tray. Pedestrians wove between the seated viewers and their game. There on the sidewalk they were forging that thick network of community with neighbors.

That sense of permanence and history is just as strong here as in rural America. For many of my neighbors, life here is life as it should be and encroaching outsiders threaten a connection to a familiar and cherished way of life. That way of life includes restaurants and grocery stands, music venues and schools, churches and other institutions that are razed or renovated in the name of progress.

Another Traditional Way of Life

Our experience suggests New Yorkers aren't constitutionally or fundamentally less friendly than anyone else. In fact, I've found that the rural value of neighborliness, for example, is no less important in the city. It just manifests in different ways.

The profound density in which we live has real consequences for the way neighbors engage. When two million people live closely together without privacy, it is actually a kindness—not a rudeness—to ignore people on the sidewalk or subway. You have to allow your neighbor to enjoy the privacy they seek in the midst of a crowd. It's like New Yorkers instinctively know Proverbs 27:14 (NLT): "A loud and cheerful greeting early in the morning will be taken as a curse!"

And we have received great kindness from strangers in times of need in the city. The Saturday the O'Brien clan was rained out during our family fun day in Central Park began well enough, with rowing in the lake.

When we got to the ticket counter to rent our boat, the cashier asked for our $15/hour rental fee (which I expected) and a $20 cash deposit (which I didn't expect). I didn't have enough cash on me and turned to slip away quickly. I was embarrassed and annoyed.

The man behind me saw what was happening and promptly handed me a $20 bill. "I know what it's like to get all the way down here with kids and . . . just take it." I thanked him profusely and told him we'd pay him back when we returned to shore.

I waited for him on the shore when we returned. When his wife saw me, she said, "Oh, you're a good person!" The husband said, "You didn't have to wait. You could have paid it forward."

This is one of several encounters we've had in this big, intimidating city, in which the people of New York have proven quite kind and hospitable. It almost makes up for the guy who threw up on the sidewalk outside our kitchen window.

One way I've tried to connect with the city is by reading books by and about authors from New York. They have done for me what Mark Twain did for Wendell Berry—they have helped make my life here "imaginable." Stories from decades past make the lives of previous New Yorkers imaginable to me, too. F. Scott Fitzgerald describes the subway experience in ways that feel remarkably contemporary. His character Amory in *This Side of Paradise* experienced "the numerous unpleasant aspects of city life without money," the first of which was riding the subway:

> There was the ghastly, stinking crush of the subway—the car cards thrusting themselves at one, leering out like dull bores who grab your arm with another story; the querulous worry as to whether some one isn't leaning on you; a man deciding not to give his seat to a woman, hating her for it; the woman hating him for not doing it; at worst a squalid phantasmagoria of breath, and old cloth on human bodies and the smells of the food men ate—at best just people—too hot or too cold, tired, worried.[7]

The subway experience that can be stifling to me was stifling already in 1920-something, and for all the same reasons. It's easy to imagine it was just as stifling before that, too. The elevator ride I take every morning at the office is given a comforting sense of precedent by E. B. White, who noted in the middle of the last century how "passengers in an elevator, whether wedged tight or scattered with room to spare" adhere to "the unwritten code" by which they all carefully avoid "any slight recognition of joint occupancy."[8]

At the very least, it is becoming clear to me that while I imagined that the way I spent my summers was a "traditional way of life," there was a traditional way of life here, too, that is just as old, just as consistent.

This lesson was confirmed one Saturday morning as I waited for my turn in the barber's chair. An older gentleman in the chair ahead of me described how he'd been coming to this barber shop for generations. "Ray has shaved me," he said. "Ray's old man has shaved me. And Ray's old man's old man has shaved me."

It is as important to my neighbors here to preserve that way of life as it is for my rural family. Even if the ways of life we're trying to preserve are very, very different.

Not the New York We Expected

We moved to New York with the single narrative that New York is a cold, hard place and that we'd be lucky to find any signs of sincere human kindness here. It would be exceedingly trite (and unhelpful for you) if we were simply to conclude that we learned upon further examination that the city wasn't so bad after all. But there is quite a bit more to it than that. *Where* we live in the city has given us a vastly different view of it than we might have gotten elsewhere. More specifically, our view of the city—and even our perceptions of our previous experience in the suburbs and my experience of life in small-town and rural America—has been challenged by the Christian community we joined in Manhattan.

When we moved to New York City, we settled in Washington Heights in Upper Manhattan. Our decision to live in Washington Heights was determined primarily by economics. I just could not imagine paying *so much rent* for *so little space* somewhere like the Upper West Side.

So, completely naively, we moved into the Heights and immediately became ethnic minorities.

Since the middle of the twentieth century, Washington Heights has been a neighborhood of immigrants. During the Second World War, Jewish immigrants made their way from Germany to the Heights to escape the horrors of the Holocaust. For a time, the part of the neighborhood my family lives in was nicknamed "Little Frankfurt." A generation later, a new wave of immigrants moved into the Heights—Caribbean populations, including Puerto Ricans but primarily Dominicans. At the height of the crack epidemic in the late 1970s and early 1980s, Jewish and Dominican activists, including devoted mothers and religious leaders, banded together to wage a grassroots war on drugs. Eventually they won, and in the '80s and '90s, waves of Dominicans moved into the neighborhood to fill vacant buildings.[9]

In addition to being white in a predominantly Dominican neighborhood, my wife and I also have two adopted children. Both of them are ethnically different from us and from each other. We are quite a sight. And we've received our fair share of stares. But the one place we feel totally normal is at church.

We worship in a new church. Our service is bilingual. The

congregation is majority Latino but very diverse. In fact, the congregation reflects the ethnic diversity of the neighborhood (60-something percent Latino and 40 percent "other"). Being surrounded by diverse families is a gift in itself for a family like ours. We've received several other gifts by worshiping in a multiethnic urban church.

One gift was a perspective on the city I had never considered. Early in our time at the church, one of our congregants preached a great sermon on Jeremiah 29:1–14. American Christians love one verse in that passage, verse 11, and it has become the life verse for graduates and people in other sorts of transition: "'For I know the plans I have for you,' declares the LORD, 'plans to prosper you and not to harm you, plans to give you hope and a future'" (NIV). Another verse in that passage is popular in literature about urban church planting and, in general, in discussions about Christian cultural engagement. Verse 7 reads: "seek the peace and prosperity of the city to which I have carried you into exile. Pray to the LORD for it, because if it prospers, you too will prosper" (NIV).

Our speaker this day spent more time on the opening verses of the passage, establishing the context of the passage as the pain and disorientation that comes from exile. The speaker was Puerto Rican, the son of immigrants. He talked about how some people come to New York City to make their break on Broadway, or to launch their publishing career, or to earn lots of money in finance for a few years so they can go live wherever they want after that. They come for opportunity—my family falls into this category.

Others are like the Hebrew exiles in Jeremiah 29 and

come to New York City for a different reason. They come because of trauma. The Jewish refugees who moved to the neighborhood during the Second World War left homes and families, many of whom didn't survive, to start over in a foreign land. The Dominican population is here, in part, because of political unrest in the Caribbean. The immigrant story is, in part, a story of exile.

In any case, these two groups of people—those who come to the city because of opportunity and those who come because of trauma—experience the neighborhood and the city very differently. In a church like ours, these two groups of people worship side by side, share Communion, and raise children together. Worshiping in a community like this has affected the way I understand my faith.

For one, I've learned that hips can be used in worship.

I've raised my hands in worship. I've bent my knees in worship. Doggone it, I've even clapped and swayed. But never before have my hips been tempted to involve themselves in worship. And it shows: they are very bad at it.

Worshiping in this context has made me aware that every other church I've ever attended has been designed to appeal to someone just like me. As much as I enjoy the Caribbean flavor of our worship, it is a constant reminder that our service and programs are not designed to reach me—they are designed to speak the heart language and meet the needs of other people in our community.

That's how it should be, of course. But it strikes me that for all of my life I've been part of churches that were actively accommodating to people just like me—people my age and my race and my socioeconomic status. And I never thought of our worship and programs as "how *we* do church." I thought of those things as "how people *ought* to do church."

The implications of this lesson don't stop with my past church experience. It's become clearer to me in recent months that the vast majority of ministry resources, even *Christian* resources more broadly, are produced with "me" in mind. And on the whole, the "me" most Christian resources target is not the urban me or the rural me, but the suburban me. (More on that later.) In any case, worshiping with this diverse community has helped me see that I've enjoyed a privileged status for a long time and never really realized it. I and people like me have held the power to shape the single story—the single story about what successful ministry looks like and what "good" worship sounds like and even the single story about immigrants and minority experiences of life and faith. The gift that comes from worshiping in a service that isn't designed for me is that it reveals the depth of my expectations and the power of the single stories I have bought into.

The gift that comes from worshiping in a service that isn't designed for me is that it reveals the depth of my expectations and the power of the single stories I have bought into.

This is not a fun lesson, but it's an important one.

We thought moving to one of the most diverse cities in America would mean that we would find comfortable diversity everywhere. Boy, were we mistaken. The longer I live in Manhattan, the more striking it is to me how segregated the city is. Neighborhoods and even blocks divide along ethnic designations. Schools can be monocultural even in diverse neighborhoods. Gentrification changes neighborhoods and creates resentment between communities. It's harder than I realized to find churches in the city that are committed to radical diversity.

Common Cause Where You Least Expect It

All our social and civic systems work against ethnic and socioeconomic integration. It's possible I knew that intellectually before now. But living where we live and worshiping where we worship has driven the point home: diversity doesn't just "happen." It takes deliberate and uncomfortable intentionality. It takes a group of people who are happy to hear all the church announcements twice—once in English and then again in Spanish—happy to sing all the songs in two languages. It takes a group of people who are willing to sacrifice their preferences so someone who sits near them can hear God speak to them the way they need to hear Him.

In doing all this, we have discovered the most surprising lesson of all. In New York City, the place I find community with a group of people who most share the rural and small-town values I grew up with—values of neighborliness and resourcefulness, commitment to faith and family and basic decency—is in an ethnic minority neighborhood. Downtown, on the Upper West Side, in Midtown, or further south, my children have been treated as nuisances on the sidewalk. Here in the Heights, my Dominican neighbors laugh when the kids rush by on their scooter and tousle their hair when they ride too close. I watch my neighbors lug rolling tool bags up and down the subway stairs to put in long days of manual labor. On the weekends, they host huge parties in the park.

The media (whatever that means) often paints the picture that rural white people and urban minorities are the two least similar populations in America. That the values gulf between them is irreparable. My experience is very much the opposite. From where I stand, I see a lot of common ground between these groups and a lot of parties with a vested interest in keeping them divided.

The other day I told my son how proud I am at how quickly he makes friends on the playground. He just walks right up and introduces himself. "I'm proud of you," I said, "because I didn't teach you to do that. I don't even know *how* to do that. I didn't have to do that sort of thing when I was a kid."

"I know, Daddy," he said. "Because you grew up in the *woods*."

While that's not entirely true, he identified the challenge. I worry about how to reinforce certain values in him and his sister when I can't replicate the experiences that instilled them in me. And yet my children are clearly learning the importance of place and neighborliness, and a kind of resourcefulness. They'll be fine. I'm the one who still has a lot to learn.

9

Common Cause in the Kingdom

Peoria, Illinois

Touching down on the runway at the Peoria, Illinois, airport evoked both warm and anxious feelings. I was scheduled to speak at a gathering for the Rural Home Mission Agency (RHMA). It was my second time and I was very eager to be back. The RHMA has a clear and compelling vision to plant and support churches in small towns and the country. Their event is energetic and well organized. And I was honored to be there, because they had adopted as the title for the conference the title of my first book, *The Strategically Small Church*.

The Strategically Small Church celebrates the unique strengths of small congregations. When I worked as an editor for *Leadership Journal* in the mid-2000s, I regularly observed a phenomenon at ministry conferences. Pastors in the audience would clap and laugh and cheer for the pastors who were speaking from the platform. The speakers were usually pastors, too, and usually led large, successful ministries. After the plenary talks I would ask attendees what they thought about the message they just heard. Their response regularly went something like this:

"That speaker is so funny and gifted. While he was talking, I was tuned in and inspired. But now that the session is over, I realize that I'll never be successful like he is. My church just doesn't have the resources he has. My town doesn't even have enough people to support a big ministry. Now that I think about it, the experience of being at this conference is actually a little demoralizing."

After hearing responses like this for several years, I researched and wrote about churches with small attendance and small budgets that were doing exciting things for the kingdom of God. The stories of ministry faithfulness in the book have resonated with pastors across the country, and I have had the opportunity to speak at events because of it.

Even so, by the time I spoke at the RHMA conference for the first time, my family had moved back (briefly) to Arkansas. And I feared I lacked credibility with this small-church crowd because at the time I was on staff at a megachurch.

This time around, my second time at the conference, I feared I lacked credibility again but for a different reason. Now we lived in Manhattan, the least rural place in America, and I had been invited to address a room full of "town and country" pastors.

This Midwestern context could not be more different from the context in which I now lived and ministered. RHMA, which plants and supports small-town and rural churches, is essentially the photographic negative of the organization for which I work, City to City. We help leaders start and strengthen churches in global cities.

The church in which we met was clean and spacious, on a campus on the edge of Peoria where town meets country. The worship space seated several hundred. In fact, during the opening worship service, it occurred to me that I had not seen this many Christians in one room in the entire first year we lived in Manhattan.

The ethnic makeup of the room was a significant change, too. We live in a neighborhood that is more than 80 percent Latino. We worship in a multiethnic church. The majority of the faces in the crowd at this conference were white. As my time to present approached, I experienced the growing fear—as I often do, when I return to rural and small-town contexts—that my time living in the city has rendered me irrelevant to "normal" people. I wanted desperately to be useful.

When the time came, I opened my first breakout session with a question designed to gauge the crowd. I asked them, "What are the most difficult challenges you face in ministry in your rural and small-town contexts?"

"Money," someone said. "We don't have the finances to offer programs or remodel the building. And our people can't afford to give any more than they give already."

"We can't attract families," someone said. "Our church is aging, because all the young couples with kids aren't just leaving the church—they're leaving the area."

"Our town is actually growing," said another. "People are moving in. But they don't have a Christian background, and they don't view the church as relevant."

Once the conversation started, it picked up steam. In the next few minutes these small-town and rural pastors voiced a number of critical challenges. Social isolation. Parishioners who suffered from addiction. Programs failing because people are always leaving. Limited resources of all sorts—financial and human alike. How do you build a church on a shrinking population? The concerns these pastors voiced echoed an observation from author and pastor Glenn Daman. "To pastor a rural church is always to struggle with having enough people, resources, or programs," Daman writes. "To pastor in rural communities is to live in the realm of obscurity and frustration, to always live with a sense of futility in ministry."[1]

It is impossible to hear these pastors describe the challenges they face in ministry and not be moved. They stand in the gap for their congregation against dire odds. But as I heard them describe the unique difficulties of town and country ministry, I felt something more than empathy. I felt a thrill of insight. Because it occurred to me then—and has been reinforced for me since—that these challenges are not unique, strictly speaking, to rural and small-town contexts. The list of challenges these pastors generated is strikingly similar to the list of challenges I was learning that *urban* pastors face. In fact, Glenn Daman's insightful and moving summary of rural ministry could just as easily apply in my Manhattan context. It could just as accurately be said that to pastor an *urban* church is always to struggle with having enough people, resources, or programs. To pastor in *urban* communities is to live in the realm of obscurity and frustration, to always live with a sense of futility in ministry.

One of the joys of my current job is meeting regularly with church planters from New York City and even around the world. In these conversations, and in the training sessions our organization offers, I am privileged to hear pastors talk transparently about the difficulties of urban ministry. Again and again, familiar themes emerge in those conversations about the city pastor's most pressing challenges:

"Money," someone will say. "The people we reach are under-resourced. They can't give more than they give. And the school we meet in just doubled our rent. We barely make ends meet." This challenge is noted by Drew Hyun, who pastors a multicampus church called Hope NYC: "Financial worries are probably the number one stressor for most church planters I meet in the city."[2]

"We can't attract families," someone else will say. "We may get them for a little while. But as soon as kids age toward high school, families move out to the suburbs. We can't keep families with kids in our church—or in our neighborhood."

"We attract people," someone might offer. "But they don't come to New York for community. They come for their jobs. And for the arts and the culture. Even if they consider church relevant, they only attend once or twice a month."

If you press them harder, these pastors will talk about the real struggle of social isolation in the city, even among Christians. Just because you live in proximity doesn't mean you are sharing life together. They will talk about addiction and poverty. They will talk about programs failing because urban people are transient. They live in the city for a couple of years, and then they move away. How do you build a church on a temporary population?

If you listen to media reports about the issues that divide these United States, you are likely to walk away with the impression that urban and rural America couldn't be more different. If you listen to the fears and frustrations of America's pastors, you quickly realize that while the lived experience of city and country people may be quite different, nevertheless, urban and rural churches have a lot more in common than they may realize.

Urban and rural churches have a lot more in common than they realize.

It is important to point out these similarities because they often go unnoticed. When urban or rural leaders describe the unique challenges of their own contexts, they often do so by comparison to the opposite context. A rural pastor might point out that he is a solo pastor with a razor-thin budget, unlike urban churches that frequently have "multiple staff members and dynamic programs."[3] An urban pastor might note how hard it is to build programs on a transient congregation, unlike in rural settings where people are settled and secure.[4]

It's as if pastors across the country feel about their ministries the way Americans feel about the places they live: that people who minister in other places don't understand the challenges they face.

The truth is, both rural and urban pastors are often, if unconsciously, comparing themselves to models of ministry most common in the suburbs. Often the speakers who headline Christian ministry conferences are pastors whose ministries have grown large and fast. The success of their ministry earns them invitations to share with other pastors how their approach to programming or preaching or discipleship can result in ministry success for other people, too. What is less often acknowledged is that America's largest churches, and therefore the leaders who pastor them, are concentrated in a couple of geographic regions. Almost half are in the South and another quarter are in the West, with a special concentration in California.[5] Moreover, megachurches are "a predominantly suburban and exurban phenomenon, locating in places accessible mostly (or only) by automobile, with ample parking, often near highway intersections."[6]

Certainly this doesn't mean a church can't grow large in a city or in the country. But statistically speaking, the majority of ministries that are celebrated as "successful" are also suburban. For this reason, suburban ministry has become the standard in ministry, and both urban and rural pastors struggle to live up to the standard. The primary reason for this is that the suburban context is characterized by opportunity. There is always more land to buy, more people to reach. Both rural and urban ministry, by contrast, are characterized by limitation.

I don't mean to imply that rural and urban contexts are *the same*. Far from it. The lived realities and local needs vary widely. My goal is not to homogenize these complex contexts nor imply that ministry is easy in the suburbs. Yet, urban and rural ministers experience similar pressures and face similar challenges, even if the causes of those pressures and the natures of those challenges are different. They are more similar to each other than to the suburban contexts that separate them.

Rural and urban pastors might feel less isolated and discouraged if they realized that other pastors in very different contexts face challenges similar to the ones they face.

I can't help but think that rural and urban pastors alike might feel less isolated and discouraged if they realized that other pastors in very different contexts face challenges similar to the ones they face. Does that mean urban and rural Christians need to unite against the common enemy of Suburbia? No. But we do share common enemies, all of us, wherever we live. All of us face powers that intentionally (and unintentionally) divide us.

We all face easy stereotypes and single stories.

We all face isolation from one another that enables us to perceive our own challenges as more severe than others' and entirely unique ... that force us to compare our ministries and even our life experiences to those of others, resulting either in feelings of superiority or inferiority.

This discussion about the way geography affects ministry implies the beginning of a solution to the issues that divide us. Pollsters and pundits would have us believe that the city and the country are the two poles of the cultural divide. But if pastors in the country can recognize that they share fears and aspirations with pastors in the city—that the challenges they face in ministry, while different in the details, are not so unlike the challenges others face—and if they can recognize and emphasize their common cause instead of their differences, then their congregations can do the same. Because the challenges pastors face are a reflection of the challenges their congregants face. If pastors can recognize their common cause in ministry, then Christians everywhere can recognize their common cause in living out their faith, wherever they live.

If pastors can recognize their common cause in ministry, then Christians everywhere can recognize their common cause in living out their faith, wherever they live.

Suburbanites have an important role to play in this work. The suburbs are, in important ways, the bridge between the city and the country. Suburbs are filled with former small-town and country folk who moved to a larger place for work or education. They are likewise filled with urbanites who retreated from the noise and hustle of the city in favor of a quieter life. The suburbs are full of relational capital that can be leveraged for the sake of Christian unity.

What I know for sure is that there is no institution in America with a vested interest in uniting the regional divisions we face except for the church of Christ. We can be part of the problem or we can be part of the solution.

10

The Flip Side

"Whoever tells you he knows everything about his own neighborhood you can be sure is fooling himself."

—Steve Katz, *Florry of Washington Heights*[1]

One evening not long ago my wife and I found ourselves discussing the old television show *The Beverly Hillbillies*. The fact that we both grew up watching the show was actually slightly more surprising than the fact that we were talking about it twenty years later. Because she grew up overseas, Amy received a random assortment of American media. *The Beverly Hillbillies* was one of those television shows that made it across the pond. Neither of us watched the show because we *liked* it. She grew up with a limited selection of American television; I grew up without cable. In the years before streaming video, you didn't only watch shows you liked. You watched shows because they were *on*.

It turns out we both disliked *The Beverly Hillbillies* but for different reasons.

When I watch *The Beverly Hillbillies*, what I see is the clear message from Hollywood, still reinforced elsewhere in American culture, that a rural Southern family can never be anything *but* white trash, no matter how much money they have. "You can take the boy out of the country," as they say, "but you can't take the country out of the boy." In that show, I see the nation laughing at a bunch of rednecks, but worse—stereotyped and stylized rednecks—a gross facsimile of people from the part of the country I grew up in. I see a reflection of myself distorted through the glass of American popular culture. The rural people I knew had their quirks, to be sure, but they weren't buffoons. *The Beverly Hillbillies* made a mockery of my childhood sanctuary.

Amy grew up in an Asian city and spent her summers back home in America, like I did, in the rural South. But while my rural summers were a refuge for me, Amy frequently felt marginalized, excluded, and mistrusted—an outsider. Her outsider status was reinforced by the small-town folks who identified her as a "city kid." And that's why, she told me, *she* has a hard time watching *The Beverly Hillbillies*—because she sees herself reflected, too, through the distorting lens of popular entertainment.

She doesn't see herself in the backwoods Clampetts, like I do. She sees herself in the city banker, Milburn Drysdale, who is so money-obsessed that he frequently makes a fool of himself. When she watches the show, she sees in it the sort of mistrust she felt from rural people during her summers in the US, a barely concealed disdain for city slickers as immoral and lazy, looking for the quick, clean way to pick your pockets. In our discussion of the issues, she pointed out that the Clampetts are the heroes and the banker is the villain.

"Sure," I admitted. "But the Clampetts are idiots. They're embarrassing."

"Yes," she said. "But they are *moral*. The banker, just by being urban, is immoral."

She's right, of course, and that point of view had never occurred to me. We can both watch the same show, even today, and experience it differently—on the same couch in the same room. We are members of the same race, the same socioeconomic class, and the same religion. We are different only in gender and, because of where we spent our childhoods, in the kinds of places that shaped us. Our experiences are entirely different. She prompted me, for the first time, to look at the conflict of values between people from different places from the point of view of an urban person.

The Limits of Our Own Stories

Stories are powerful. By telling our stories, through a book like this one or across a dinner table, we feel represented and given a voice or else feel more empathetic about people who are unlike us. There's something universal about being specific.

Even so, personal narrative has significant limitations. The major one in this book is this: everything I've said up to this point about rural, small-town, suburban, and urban America is, of course, all the product of my own perspective, my own point of view. At one point in the process of telling these stories, the great challenge and truth hit me—all of this has been only from my own experience. There are people who graduated high school with me who could read all these

149

stories and say, "That wasn't my experience at all." And we'd both be right.

I have experienced all of life, in fact, as a white male from a lower middle class (now solidly middle class) point of view. Looking at some of the places I've lived from different points of view gives a very different picture of things. My wife, the city girl, for example, is not the only person who has had a negative experience in rural America. Research suggests that perceptions of life in rural America vary based on a person's race.

It's useful to acknowledge this point because it illustrates a challenge everyone has. We all normalize our own experiences of a place. Without thinking about it, we assess and evaluate places based not on any objective criteria—such as history or statistics—but on our feelings of and experiences with the places. We determine that a place is whatever we experience it to be. Lake Bistineau was peaceful, life giving, and safe for me. It provided my "comforting sense of precedent." So, for me, it is objectively wonderful because that's how I experienced it. My neighborhood is safe, not if the crime rate is low, but if I *feel* safe there. It's dangerous, not if the crime rate is high, but if I *feel* afraid. The neighborhood is culturally dynamic if it has the kinds of restaurants I like, the kind of art I consider valuable, the kind of music I prefer.

It never occurred to me, for example, that the experience of African Americans on and around Lake Bistineau might have been different from mine. But studies suggest that's the case. Although "rural Americans are more likely to see their communities as neighborly, safer and having better public schools than people in large cities, those opinions come with wide racial disparities." Values often identified as "rural values" are actually not shared equally by white people and people of color. Twenty percent fewer black people say "their area is an excellent or good place to raise children." Black respondents rate their rural communities 25 percentage points lower in the category of safety. Black rural Americans are 30 percent less likely to say that people look out for each other in rural communities. Hispanics rate rural America somewhere between black and white respondents.[2] Commentators have noted that one place black Americans feel least secure is in America's predominantly white suburbs.[3]

Which is all to say, of course, that different people can experience the same place in different ways. This is obvious in a large and diverse city like New York. Having access to multiple points of view is one gift available to the person living in a large city. With very little effort, just by walking out the door, in fact, it is obvious to me that there are lots of different people in the world who have very different points of view than I have. One of the values of the small-town and rural community, as American sociologist Robert Wuthnow has pointed out, is that in a small place people say they "know everyone." This is, of course, an illusion or hyperbole. What they mean is that while they don't know everyone, they can reasonably expect everyone in town (even the people they don't know) to share the same perspective on important issues. It's impossible to feel this way in a city. Maybe that's why the narrator of the novel *Florry of Washington Heights* begins his story the way he does. "Whoever tells you he knows everything about his own neighborhood you can be sure is fooling himself," he says. "Something else always goes on in the schoolyard while you sit on the park wall, or vice versa." He concludes, "To have the illusion that you can understand the world you've got to come from a small town."[4]

This is important to point out because parts of our country are so monocultural that it might not occur to people that others in their community experience it differently than they do. More than 30 percent of counties in America are more than 90 percent white.[5] In those places, a person who is white will have to work hard to consider their place from the point of view of someone who isn't.

I can relate. My childhood gave me very little practice navigating cross-cultural relationships. Encounters with ethnic minorities were very different in Arkansas and Louisiana. With my grandparents at the lake, my experience was extremely segregated. There were no black residents on the cul-de-sac where my grandparents lived. Occasionally we passed solitary black fishermen on the lake, but I don't recall seeing black *families* boating and skiing. Grocery stores provided a cross-section of the population, as did some fast food restaurants and the hardware store. But sit-down restaurants, churches, and other establishments seemed specified by race.

We don't have the full picture even of our own time and place. We can't get the full picture on our own. We can't look deep into ourselves to find the answers. We have to look out. It takes a great deal of effort and humility—more, frankly, than I often feel the capacity for. It takes a great deal of courage, and I feel my courage waning. It takes—perhaps easiest of all—switching off and ignoring the messages of those political parties that want to keep us alienated from each other. Instead, we need to learn from each other. We can't know our whole country on our own. If we look at things only from the point of view of our own group, we can't even fully understand our own town without the input of others.

Seeing things from someone else's point of view is harder than it sounds. It doesn't happen by accident. You have to do it on purpose.

Seeing things from someone else's point of view is harder than it sounds. For one, it doesn't happen by accident. You have to do it on purpose. But it can start with efforts as small as intentional conversations, and the results can be beautiful.

Jamal and Me and a Cabin in the Woods

A friend of mine in Manhattan (I'll call him Jamal) is a pastor in the neighborhood he grew up in. He and I are different in every conceivable way. He grew up in a dangerous neighborhood during the crack epidemic of the 1980s and early 1990s. I grew up in a small town in a rural state. He's Afro-Latino. I'm as white as a person can be. He's a talented hip-hop artist. I am not. Despite our different backgrounds, we've discovered through simple conversations that we have a lot in common.

One morning over breakfast we discovered, for example, that we agree a diner is judged on the merits of its bacon. And most diners get the bacon wrong.

After further conversation we discovered we share a vision for our future. Jamal told me in confidential tones, "Someday

I want to own a cabin in the woods—not totally off-grid but out there where it's quiet and you can think. And I want to grow my beard out long and just *be*."

"You won't believe this," I told him, "but it sounds like you've been reading my diary. Add a yard full of clucking hens and you've just described my retirement plan exactly."

From my point of view, my own desire to retire in the wilderness makes sense. Rural summers were my happy place. Why wouldn't I want to re-create those moments in my twilight years? Jamal's desire to retreat to the woods struck me as more surprising. It just goes to show you that no matter how profound an influence your place of origin may have on you, it doesn't have to determine your future.

No matter how profound an influence your place of origin may have on you, it doesn't have to determine your future.

Bonding over bacon and a shared dream of cabin living are fairly superficial connections, even if one of them is somewhat surprising. Even so, sharing transparently about our aspirations eventually led to sharing transparently about our fears. After we paid and stepped out onto the sidewalk, Jamal said, "I don't tell a lot of people about my dream of living in a cabin in the woods."

"Why's that?" I asked.

"Because I don't just want to live in a cabin. I also want to learn to hunt. But people get nervous when a guy like me starts talking about guns."

I didn't know what to say. He continued.

"I just wish more people realized that when a black man

from the hood wants to buy a gun, it's not always to shoot up the streets or rob a liquor store."

"Now that you mention it," I said, "I wish more people realized that when a white man from the country wants to buy a gun, it's not just to form a militia or resurrect the Confederacy."

After a moment we laughed and hugged and said good-bye. We were an unlikely pair that morning. A black man from the hood and a white man from the woods who had shared, at least in small ways, both simple preferences and deep aspirations. I can't speak for him, but I left our time together seeing the world differently.

Seeing things from someone else's point of view is ultimately an act of repentance. It requires admitting that I didn't see things completely before, and now I see them more clearly. And in light of the new information that I have, I'm going to think and behave differently. Christians should be prepared to spot these lapses in our perception. If we believe our human nature is so corrupted by sin and that we are prone to selfishness and self-absorption, then it's no stretch to admit that we are also, therefore, prone to see what we want to see and to filter our experiences in terms of what's best for us. We should welcome new information and the experiences of others that discipline and challenge our own experiences *precisely because* we are Christians. We should be grateful for the ministry of people who are unlike us, who can point out where we've misperceived reality and how we can make corrections. We should delight in repentance because it makes us more fully aware of God and ourselves and others.

It might strike you as odd to think of a change of perspective as an act of repentance. If we think of repentance as a response only to grievous sin, then simply "being wrong" might not require repentance. I like how Pastor Timothy Keller describes repentance motivated by the power of the gospel. "In the gospel," he explains, "the purpose of repentance is to repeatedly tap into the joy of our union with Christ to weaken our impulse to do anything contrary to God's heart."[6] In other words, repentance springs from a desire to see things the way God sees them and to act according to His will. God wants His children to "dwell in unity," not only in person but in their hearts as the united body of Christ (Psalm 133).

> *We should welcome new information and the experiences of others that discipline and challenge our own experiences* **precisely because *we are Christians.***

Dwelling in unity is a nice idea, until you try to do it. If you do, you quickly realize it's hard work. Unity requires sacrifice and discomfort and humility. Making room for someone else's experiences and perspective forces us to confront truths about ourselves that can be uncomfortable. Thankfully, on the other side of that discomfort—and, indeed, what brings us through it—is God's grace. In that sense, the places we live and the people we meet are like sacraments: opportunities to experience God's grace and mercy anew.

Check Your Mirrors

"Grandma, does God live in the city?"
I ask one morning at breakfast.
"Yes, God is here," she says.
"You just have to know where to look."

—Jennifer Grant, *Maybe God Is Like That Too*[1]

Twice in one week, just weeks before our one-year anniversary in New York, strangers rebuked my bad manners. And not just any strangers either, but rude New Yorkers. If that don't beat all.

The first time was in a library. I sat at a table designated for "quiet conversation" so I could listen in to a conference call for work and contribute—quietly—if necessary. There's no question talking was permitted here. I read and reread the placard on the table a half dozen times to be sure. I'm as committed to being quiet in the library as the next guy.

A few minutes into the call, I spoke briefly. With the microphone of my headphone speaker between thumb and forefinger, I spoke into my cupped hand like a Secret Service agent. This was covert stuff. And almost before I finished speaking, a fellow library patron hissed at me in an angry librarian whisper:

"*Sssssir*! This table is designated for quiet conversation."

"Yes, ma'am," I began, but she cut me off with a snap:

"And *that* was *not* very quiet." I spent the rest of the conference call huddled in the staircase outside the reading room door, seething quietly and secretly hoping the old woman who shushed me would see my extreme efforts to be quiet.

The other time was at a bus stop.

Most of us at the bus stop carried grocery bags from the store across the street. Only one or two people sat in the bus stop, while the rest of us trailed along the sidewalk with a wide radius of personal space between us. It was spring, and the trees above were full of pink buds but not enough leaves to cast shadows. Having been closed up in small spaces all winter, we all stood with our faces to the sun, soaking in the rays like turtles on a log.

The previous summer I learned that Manhattan's buses are a more civilized and better air-conditioned alternative to the subway. It takes sometimes twice as long by bus, but longer travel time is a small price to pay to avoid the pressing and sweating and subterranean dark of the subway system. After a long season of short daylight hours and underground commuting, I was beginning to feel like a mole-person. I craved sunlight through the bus windows and a leisurely ride home. Besides, bus people are kinder and less in a hurry, on the whole.

A man in a wheelchair was parked near the curb. The buses have ramps they can lower or extend (I had never seen it operate before) to allow wheelchairs access. I was glad

I'd see how that process worked. There was a woman surrounded by a few children nearby. The rest of us were alone together, waiting.

Soon enough the bus pulled in and stopped, and the door opened. No one moved. Usually when a door opens in Manhattan, especially on the subway, people charge to enter it, as if there's a fire or a swarm of poisonous insects behind them. But for long seconds no one budged. I took a step forward to look into the bus to see what was going on. I realized immediately that the driver was lowering the wheelchair ramp—up and out and down like a protractor. The process takes a while.

Peeking in to see what was happening meant I stepped momentarily in front of the man in the wheelchair. The woman with the children interpreted this recon effort as a maneuver to beat an elderly man to the best seat on the bus.

"Ex*cuse* me," she said. "The handicapped board first. It's just polite."

I nodded and smiled and stepped back to my place on the sidewalk. I bristled a little at her rebuke but let it go. I apologized to the man in the wheelchair. He was not offended. Everyone was silent a moment.

"I mean, we *all* want to get on the bus," the woman continued, speaking loudly enough to be heard by everyone. "But you *always* let the disabled and elderly board first. It's only polite. We have to wait our turn."

"My mistake," I said. Another quiet moment passed. I read the advertisement on the side of the bus.

"I don't mean to be *rude*," she said (as people do when

they aim to be rude), "but it's just common courtesy to let the handicapped—"

I interrupted. I shouldn't have. I should've let it go. But I didn't: "Lady, I don't need a lesson in manners."

Obviously.

She smiled, both indignant and satisfied, no doubt, at her public stand for common decency. Of the dozen or so of us on the curb, she was the only one who spoke—loudly, it seemed to me—to her children.

"Now we'll get on the bus after the two wheelchairs and after all the elderly people and everyone in front of us. We have to wait our turn. That's how we be polite."

My new strategy was to out-polite her. This was no easy task as she invited several people—people beside her and behind her—to please board the bus ahead of her. But I can be persistent. I waited until everyone was on board before I moved a muscle. When she and her children neared the bus, I waved them on: "Please," I told her, "after you. I insist."

The bus traveled west to Riverside Drive, then north. The woman and her kids rode for several stops. Each time the bus stopped to let new passengers board, she renewed her campaign of politeness. "Now if an elderly person gets on," she said, "we'll give them our seat because that's what we do. It's considerate."

Perhaps it is natural that our little interaction rubbed me the wrong way. She was quite rude, even though I was obviously the villain in her story. What wasn't natural—or at the very least, what took me by surprise—is that our little interaction, together with my experience in the library, stayed with me for weeks. For weeks when I thought about being shushed for talking or chastised for breaking mass transit protocol, I got angry and indignant. Never have I nursed a slight so long. And I couldn't understand why.

Eventually I realized that my inner moralist was offended by the implication that I—of all people—should need a lesson in manners from New Yorkers—of all people. I had never verbalized this, but apparently I like to think, as a small-town Southern transplant to the "godless east coast," that I don't need a lesson in manners from self-righteous strangers. *I* know how to be a person, thank you very much. I don't need a lesson from the likes of *you*.

Whew.

Eventually I recognized that (what I perceived as) the self-righteousness of strangers woke and angered the self-righteousness in me. The question I couldn't answer was, why had it never happened before? Why now? What's different?

There's a metaphor that has helped me make sense of it.

All My Flaws Way Up Close

There's a type of mirror I associate with my grandmother's house and hotel bathrooms. It's round and sometimes attached to the end of a telescoping arm mounted on the wall. Some of them (horror of horrors) have a light that enhances their effect. These are mirrors for people who have a higher tolerance than I have for facing the truth about their physical imperfections. They are makeup mirrors.

One side of the mirror reflects your face at its normal size.

The other side of the mirror reflects at double magnification or more. Inside that magnifying surface is another mirror still, a half-dollar sized surface that reflects your features at a truly disturbing level of magnification.

The lens that simply reflects at normal size is fine. It's just a normal mirror. It shows you what you see in any reflective surface, from your car's rearview mirror to a toaster.

The other two surfaces are horrific. They expose and amplify parts of your face you don't normally see, at least not in great detail. The little imperfections: stray hairs, dark spots, wrinkles. All of them leap out at you in enormous dimensions. A small hair becomes a shaft of pencil lead. A wrinkle becomes a dry creek bed. A freckle becomes a liver spot. Every pore is a monstrosity. And that's just the second lens. The third lens—heaven help us.

Most disturbing, of course, is that these mirrors don't *add* these imperfections to our faces. They merely expose them. Neither do they expose them gently or tactfully. Instead, they magnify your faults and flaws until your faults and flaws are all you can see. That's sort of the point of the mirror, though. It presents these faults and flaws so you can deal with them: pluck them, fill them, or cover them up.

My theory is that different places reflect our image back to us in much the same way, at different levels of magnification. Our hometown or place of origin mirrors back to us the "us" we see most frequently. It shows us the person we see most often. Certainly there are blemishes and imperfections, but they are the ones we are aware of and have either accepted or addressed or have become good at concealing.

When you move to a new place, it's like flipping the mirror. In an unfamiliar place, qualities and characteristics that you don't normally see suddenly are

When you move to a new place, it's like flipping the mirror. Parts of you that you don't normally see suddenly are projected back to you with alarming clarity.

projected back to you with alarming clarity. Personality traits, weaknesses, and even strengths are magnified. Sometimes this process of discovery is encouraging. College students, for example, often discover hidden talents or passions during their university years. They realize they enjoy or are good at things they would never have experienced in their home community. Sometimes, though, this process of discovery is discouraging. In high school I considered myself a pretty good guitar player. At college I realized half the incoming freshman class played guitar, and I didn't play any better than most of them. My new context reflected back my image in a way I hadn't seen it. This realization didn't devastate me. I was glad for a more objective outlook on my talents.

But some new places are like that third mirror, the little terrible one that magnifies exponentially. The images these contexts send back to you can be deeply distressing or disorienting. Some contexts press you and reveal deep insecurities or limitations. They bring buried flaws—flaws you didn't even know you should try to conceal—into sharp focus.

New York City has been an ultra-magnifying mirror for me. The density and diversity and hurry and noise and all that has highlighted features of my personality that I wasn't aware of before and frankly am not crazy about. Never before now did I recognize a self-righteous streak in myself. Perhaps it's new. But I doubt it. I suspect what's happened is that it's always been there, and I've been able either to manage it or to conceal it in the places I lived before. Here that feature of my personality is magnified and the mirror is so constantly before me that I can't forget what I look like, and I can't simply cover it up.

While the effects are certainly most powerful and least escapable when you are immersed in a new context, you can encounter new contexts without relocating geographically. In some ways, the American media provides something like a mirror of different places. We are presented with different places when we watch the news or scroll through social media feeds. If we're willing to let them, these experiences can help us deal with our hidden flaws.

I can't help but think that one of the reasons Americans from different places cast one another in such negative light is because we reflect back to one another the limits and flaws of our respective value systems. Urban America (via news and social media) portrays rural America as racist and misogynistic. Perhaps part of the reason is because the racism and misogyny urbanites believe they see in rural America reflects back to them the racism and misogyny of urban America. These two things—racism and misogyny—are entirely incompatible with urban, often liberal, values. And so its presence in someone else reflects it back to them. And they despise it.

Rural America is known for its hospitality and neighborliness. Perhaps part of the reason rural Americans are so incensed about immigration, which is frequently welcomed in cities, is because it reflects back to rural America the limits of its hospitality and neighborliness. All of this is to say that the experiences of other people from our own contexts can hold up a mirror to us, too. And perhaps this is at least part of the source of our resentment for one another.

> *The experiences of other people from our own contexts can hold up a mirror to us. Perhaps this is at least part of the source of our resentment for one another.*

Fortunately there is a spiritual discipline that can provide a helpful process for dealing with the feelings and flaws that an encounter with another "place" reflects back to us. The practice is called the "daily examen," and it's a way to check our mirrors.

**CHECKING OUR MIRRORS:
THE DAILY EXAMEN**

The daily examen is described a variety of ways, and none of them are specifically intended for helping us process the disorientation of a cross-cultural experience. So the version presented here is adapted to meet the needs of this book. The basic elements are these:[2]

STILLNESS. Become quiet and acknowledging God's presence with you in the moment.

GRATITUDE. Review the day and give thanks for God's many blessings, large and small: the kindness of a stranger, a promotion at work, a word of encouragement from a friend.

REFLECTION. Consider the motives and attitudes that drove your actions during the day. Pay attention to your emotions. Say, for example, you were rude to a stranger on a city bus. Spend some time reflecting on why.

REPENTANCE. Acknowledge sinful motives and behaviors to God. And thank Him for His forgiveness. He knew your motives before you did, and He loved you anyway.

HOPEFULNESS. Ask God for grace to operate more faithfully tomorrow.

I've found this practice to be a special means of grace in my Christian life in general, a way God uses to help me recognize the depth of my sin and receive His forgiveness. When I practice it regularly, I have a greater sense of peace and a greater sense of God's presence. It truly is a gift.

And it was the way I realized that my problem with the library patron and the woman on the bus was, ultimately, a problem with *myself* and not a problem with them. Here's how the examen works, applied to working through my feelings about living in or visiting or otherwise encountering a new place:

1. **Become aware of God's presence.** I find a quiet place and calm down. Most of the time, I do this in bed before I fall asleep because there's little else to distract me. The kids are asleep. The lights are off. I breathe and focus. Often it takes me a few minutes to calm racing thoughts or silence problems from the day that I'm still trying to solve. My goal is to recognize that God is with me wherever I am, even when I feel the most alone. Even in some big, secular city. Even in some backwater town in the middle of nowhere.

2. **Give thanks for God's blessings.** When I feel focused and assured of God's presence, I reflect on the day and make an effort to recognize the good things God has done for me. One night I recalled the man who gave me $20 in Central Park so I could take my family rowing; another night, the young woman who spoke encouraging words to my son at a deli counter. These are all small graces from God mediated by strangers. I thank Him for these experiences.

3. **Review the day and pay attention to your emotions.** From this posture of gratitude, I then think over what happened today and how I responded. Often a particular situation stands out among the others. I ask myself, "Why did I respond the way I did?" In the library and on the bus, I responded to a rebuke from strangers with deep and immediate indignation. Why? Because I pride myself on being polite and respectful, as I was taught to be in small-town

America. And it bothered me to think that people I was taught to consider rude—New Yorkers—might consider *me* rude. In short, my self-righteousness was exposed by words from strangers. And I didn't like what I saw.

4. **Repent and receive forgiveness.** Next I confess whatever sin God brings to mind during this time of reflection. After reflecting on my interactions with the woman at the library and the woman on the bus, I confess my self-righteousness. The only person who isn't aware of it is me, anyway. God knows about it. My wife knows about it. My kids know about it. And the thing is, God and my family know about my self-righteousness and love me anyway. So I receive His forgiveness—acknowledge, really, the forgiveness I've already received in Christ—and release my right to continue to be self-righteous.

5. **Give thanks for God's grace to have a better tomorrow.** I end with a prayer of thanksgiving: "Thank You, God, that You know my innermost parts and love me anyway. Help me to face the day tomorrow—which has the same uncertainties and stressors and pressures as today—with a spirit of humility and compassion that is made possible only by Your Holy Spirit."

The city exerts a constant and profound pressure that is still new to me. Busyness, density, diversity, lack of privacy and personal space—together these things press and squeeze, and sometimes what comes out of me is ugly. I need to constantly check my mirrors. The thing is, living in small-town Arkansas had a similar effect on my wife. The culture was foreign enough for her that it revealed things she needed to confess and leave before God in repentance. For those of us living somewhere we didn't grow up, our new place doesn't so much change us as it reveals what's always been there but kept hidden. If we don't want to be like the unfaithful disciple described in the book of James, the man who looks at himself in the mirror and immediately forgets what he looks like, we have to learn to bring those lessons before the Lord in prayer (James 1:23–24). In fact, God invites us to "look intently" into the perfect law of God, the Bible, to let it reflect all our imperfections so we can ultimately be transformed into the image of Christ (1:25 NASB). In this sense, God uses difficult places to help transform us into His image. It isn't always easy. But it's good.

12

Pray Like It's Your Sacred Place

"For the sake of my brothers and my friends,
I will now say, 'May peace be within you.'"

—Psalm 122:8 NASB

Sometime in elementary school, one of my classmates was giving me grief. He wasn't a bully, but he irked me and I complained about him at home. My mom encouraged me to pray for him. So we did. And before too long my heart changed toward him. I became more empathetic, more patient. Instead of being frustrated by him, I *felt for* him.

All of this change was much to my disappointment, I should add.

Praying for someone can change our feelings about them. The Bible suggests that praying for some *place* can likewise change our feelings about that place and the people who live there.

The Spirituality of Two Cities

Psalm 122 is one of the fifteen "Songs of Ascent" in the book of Psalms. Scholars assume that these were songs pilgrims sang on their walk to Jerusalem for religious festivals that were held there. Jesus goes "up to Jerusalem" three times in the book of John (2:13; 5:1; 12:12 NASB). Maybe as He walked with His disciples along the way, they sang these very songs together. Maybe it was one of these songs that Jesus and His disciples sang after they celebrated Passover, just before heading to the Mount of Olives (Matt. 26:30).

Many years before Jesus sang these songs, travelers who had journeyed far and returned would have sung them. Exiles who returned from captivity would have also sung them. Psalm 122 celebrates the moment of arriving in Jerusalem— "Our feet are standing within your gates, O Jerusalem"—and heading for the temple to worship—"I was glad when they said to me, 'Let us go to the house of the LORD'" (NASB). The psalm goes on to explain the enthusiasm the psalmist felt for the city of David. Jerusalem represented God's rule and reign, both in the temple and in the "thrones of the house of David." It was the bastion for God's law and justice.

Eugene Peterson describes the city's significance beautifully:

> In Jerusalem everything that God said was remembered and celebrated. When you went to Jerusalem, you encountered the great foundational realities: God created you, God redeemed you, God provided for you. In Jerusalem

you saw in ritual and heard proclaimed in preaching that powerful history-shaping truth that God forgives our sins and makes it possible to live without guilt and with purpose. In Jerusalem all the scattered fragments of experience, all the bits and pieces of truth and feeling and perception were put together in a single whole.[1]

It was the one place on earth where everything should be right and good for the people of Israel. That's why the psalmist encourages the singers of his song to "pray for the peace of Jerusalem!" That great city was a sign of God's kingdom on earth. If Jerusalem prospered, the whole world prospered with it, by God's providence. King David himself had prayed that God would build up the walls of Jerusalem. He concludes his famous prayer of confession in Psalm 51 with a prayer for the holy city. "Do good to Zion in your good pleasure," he asked of God; "build up the walls of Jerusalem" (51:18). Included in that prosperity, of course, were all those who loved Jerusalem, who understood what it represented. So, "for my brother's and companions' sake," the psalmist prayed for the peace and prosperity in the city of God. He will seek its good. If it prospers, they prosper.

If Jerusalem represented all that was right and good, Babylon represented the opposite. Babylon stood in total opposition to God and His plans in every way. It was morally corrupt—and corrupting. It had its own gods, and it defied Israel's God. Instead of representing the rule and reign of God, Babylon represented injustice and oppression. The Israelites who lived there did not march there with Songs of Ascent on their lips; they limped there in long slave caravans. They were not drawn by a vision of the holy city before them. They were driven by captors behind them. For as long as they lived in Babylon, for generations, exiled Israelites longed to return to Jerusalem.

Their feelings are captured powerfully in another song, Psalm 137.

The psalm begins on a sorrowful note. The singer is exiled in a foreign land. He has gathered with friends by the river. There, by "the waters of Babylon," he and his countrymen "sat down and wept, when [they] remembered Zion" (137:1). God's presence seemed so far away. To add insult to injury, the people who took these singers captive taunted them by saying, "Sing us one of the songs of Zion!" (137:3).

And there on the banks of strange waters, instead of offering a prayer of blessing for Babylon, as they had for Jerusalem, they vent their frustration in an angry curse: "O daughter of Babylon, doomed to be destroyed, blessed shall he be who repays you with what you have done to us!" (137:8).

What were the exiled children of God supposed to *do* with these feelings of vengeance, far from home weeping and awaiting God's deliverance? God commanded them in the book of Jeremiah to do the same thing for their enemies that my mom encouraged me to do with mine, the same thing Jesus commanded His disciples to do: pray for them.

Through Jeremiah the prophet, God instructs His people in Babylon, for as long as they live in that great city, to make a life there. Get comfortable. Build houses and plant vineyards and have children (Jer. 29:4–6). Don't just survive there, *thrive* there. And though the people's instinct is to call down curses upon their captors, God commands them to pray that Babylon will be blessed. Much as the psalmist encouraged pilgrims to pray for Jerusalem to prosper, God urges the people to "seek the welfare of the city where I have sent you into exile, and *pray to the LORD on its behalf*, for in its welfare you will find your welfare" (Jer. 29:7).

In other words, God is saying, don't just pray for Babylon. Pray for it *in the same way* that you pray for Jerusalem. Don't pray that its walls will be destroyed and its temples will be razed to the ground. Pray instead that its walls will be strong and that its laws will be just and that its people will prosper. Don't pray that the people who live there will finally meet their doom or face their day of judgment. Don't pray that God would bring ruin because of the people's sin. Pray for salvation. Pray for prosperity. Pray for that city as if it were the city of God.

Another prophet learned a similar lesson a harder way. God gave Jonah the task of preaching a message of repentance to Israel's political enemies, the Ninevites. It was the same message other prophets preached to the Israelites: repent of your sins and God will save you. Jonah didn't want to preach this good news to the Ninevites because he couldn't bear the thought of God extending mercy to them. Pastor Timothy Keller points out, "unlike the prophets Amos and Hosea, who criticized the royal administration" of King Jeroboam II "for its injustice and unfaithfulness, Jonah had supported Jeroboam's aggressive military policy to extend the nation's power and influence."[2] That is, Jonah viewed Nineveh not only as a religious rival but also as his political enemy. "The original readers of the book of Jonah," Keller continues, "would have remembered him [Jonah] as intensely patriotic, a highly partisan nationalist."[3] And now God was sending him to Israel's greatest military rival not to call down judgment upon them but to offer them the gift of forgiveness.

God was asking Jonah to treat his political enemies exactly the same way he would have treated his Israelite brothers and sisters. To love them enough to preach the good news of God's forgiveness to them. To seek, at the deepest possible level, the peace and prosperity of that great city. Jonah didn't want to. In fact, after he preached to them and they repented, he left the city and climbed a hill to watch from a distance what would happen. He expected—and hoped!—to see fire rain down from heaven. He expected to see neighboring raiders tear down the walls. Instead, God scolded Jonah for his lack of charity. He wanted Jonah to want for Nineveh what Jonah wanted for Jerusalem: forgiveness, peace, and prosperity.

America's Jerusalems and Babylons

America has no biblical Jerusalem or Babylon. There is no region of the United States in which God's presence resides permanently or especially, and there is no region of the country that officially arrays itself against God and His people. Even so, Jerusalem and Babylon are helpful as symbolic places in a discussion about what divides us.

For example, throughout my childhood, I frequently heard people refer to rural and small-town places as "God's country." And everyone knew the big cities were rife with sin. From our point of view, rural America was Jerusalem, and cities were Babylon.

Urbanites might frame the conversation in different terms but with essentially the same result. City dwellers might view themselves as progressive on important social issues, as being on the "right side of history." Rural and small-town places, by contrast, might be considered backward and even oppressive. For urbanites, the city is Jerusalem, and rural places are Babylon.

Here's why all this matters: I've lived in enough places and talked to enough people to believe that many Christians in America, whether they realize it or not, privilege their regional identity over their Christian identity. A Christian who lives in the suburbs, for example, may have greater affinity with a non-Christian who lives in the suburbs than with a Christian who lives in the country. That is, their *suburban* values may have greater impact than their *Christian* values on any number of important decisions they make. To offer just one example, evangelicals voted differently in the 2016 election depending on where they lived. Nearly three-fourths of evangelicals living in rural areas voted for Donald Trump, whereas half of evangelicals living in cities voted for Hillary Clinton. Suburban evangelicals were almost evenly divided between the two leading candidates.[4] Which is to say that where a Christian *lived* was at least as significant a determiner of how they voted as was their identity as a Christian.

Christians in America are divided over which places are Jerusalem and which are Babylon.

If this is the case, I believe God is calling Christians to begin healing the rift between our divided communities by praying, first, for the peace and prosperity of fellow Christians who live in a part of the country we may dislike. Doing so will likely mean that we have to pray for someone who is our Christian brother or sister but, at the same time, our political rival. It will likely mean that we have to pray for someone whose daily life and rhythms are unimaginable to us. If we want to see healing in the country's regional divide *in general*, we must first commit to imitate Jesus by choosing reconciliation over judgment within the household of faith.

A good first step in this direction is to pray for the peace of fellow Christians who live in an area as different from yours as Arkansas is from Manhattan (although this place could even be the pew on the other side of your church). And God has given us a template.

Take a moment now and pray for that place. You know the one. Pray for it like this:

> May those who love that place feel and be secure.
> May there be peace within its walls and security within
>   its borders.
> For the sake of my family and friends [and fellow
>   Americans], I will say,
> "Peace be within you." (adapted from Ps. 122:6–8)

It seems to me that God has not left open to Christians the option of despising any place or any people and desiring their demise. Instead, the Christian tradition and the

Christian Scriptures testify to an opposite impulse, a command that needs to become a habit in our hearts: that we pray for and seek the prosperity of both friends and enemies alike.

There are many more things we might do and probably should do. But let's begin with prayer and see if God doesn't change our hearts.

13

Taller and Fatter

Conclusion

There are at least two ways to outgrow something. One way is to get taller. Another way is to get fatter.

Getting taller is acceptable. Everyone celebrates when you get taller. "My goodness, look how tall you're getting!" they say. "Look at my boy!" they say, "Can you believe how tall he's getting?" Getting fatter, on the other hand, is regrettable. People are less likely to point it out, but they find ways. "Put on a little weight, have you?" Or, "Your wife is certainly feeding you well."

Outgrowing something—pants, for example—by getting taller implies that the thing you've outgrown has become insufficient in light of your increasing maturity. You're going places—growing up—and the thing you've outgrown can't keep up with the progress.

Outgrowing something by getting fatter implies that the thing you've outgrown is entirely sufficient but that *you* have become deficient in some way. You have become literally unfit for the thing you've outgrown.

What in the world are we talking about right now?

It seems to me that those of us who move away from the place we grew up in—the 20 percent of us who live far away from our parents—typically talk about outgrowing the place in the first sense (getting taller). We matured and realized that the place wasn't going to grow to fit us. We had to leave.

At the same time, it seems to me that the people who stay there view us as having outgrown the place in the second sense (getting fatter). We've changed, and not for the better. Our hometowns are perfectly fine, but we've become unfit for them.

We got fatter, not taller.

This is, of course, my great fear as someone who grew up in rural America and now lives in Manhattan. That living where I live will put such distance between myself and my hometown that I'll forget where I came from. That my children won't grow up with the same values as my family. That I've not only made myself unfit, but I've implicated future generations as well. A relative of mine reinforced this fear during a trip to visit family.

I was thumbing through an interesting series of books on her shelf, a collection of guidebooks for traditional skills and recipes—like basket weaving and curing meat.

"You might oughta get yourself a set of those," she said. "Living in New York, you'll forget how to do anything practical."

A Third Way

Over the last century, America has transitioned from a predominantly rural nation to a predominantly urban (or suburban) nation. Some will say this transition from rural to urban is natural maturity, and we are simply leaving behind a way of life that doesn't suit us anymore. Some Americans view this transition as getting taller.

Others view this transition as getting fatter. They see the changes and can't help but think that we've abandoned the values that made us great. We don't know how to do "anything practical" anymore. As a people, we are fast becoming unfit for our great country.

I feel this tension in myself, as I've mentioned. And I feel it in our populace. I feel it in the church. Because Christians are just as divided as other Americans about whether or not these changes are positive or negative. The reason for this, I suspect, is because most Christians in America derive a primary sense of identity from where they live.

If our primary sense of identity comes from where we live, then our perspective on the country and its regions will be shaped by our geography more than by our faith. Rural and suburban and urban Christians may dislike each other because, instead of being *Christians* first and foremost, they are in fact *rural* or *suburban* or *urban* first and foremost. If our primary sense of identity is our geography—or our politics or our class or status—then the church should never expect to rise above the divisions that separate the rest of the country. In fact, we will likely baptize

If our primary sense of identity is our geography—or politics, class, status—then the church should never expect to rise above the divisions that separate the rest of the country.

those differences and place spiritual value on our regional opinions. We will feel increasingly distrusting of, and mistrusted by, our fellow Christians.

Fortunately, Christians are called to find their primary identity in something else. In some*one* else: in Christ.

If we place our primary identity in Christ, we have new options available to us that the rest of our countrymen do not have available to them. If we find our primary identity in Christ, then we can acknowledge that every place has its blind spots. Every place makes its own mistakes. And every place has its unique strengths. This is a massive overgeneralization, but hear it out: rural Christians have a tendency to resist culture. Suburban Christians tend to demand a voice in cultural conversations. Urban Christians tend to feel swallowed up by the culture, eager to be accepted but operating largely at the margins. And the truth is that each of these postures has strengths and each one has advantages. We are all right. And we are all wrong.

> *Our highest calling is not to conform to the values of the place we live in but to be progressively transformed into the image of Christ.*

If we find our primary identity in Christ, we can admit that our highest calling is not to conform to the values of the place we live in but to be progressively transformed into the image of Christ. That is, we have a fixed and shared point of reference, which isn't urban, suburban, or rural. It is Jesus.

So what's the solution? There isn't an easy answer. There are no easy answers to difficult questions. But there is a way forward. And the way forward, while it isn't easy, is simple. It is fellowship. Courageous, humble, vulnerable fellowship. Instead of adopting the culture's method of entrenching as tribes and lobbing bombs at "the other side" from a distance, we have to make a concerted effort to come close to those with whom we disagree. We have to have honest conversations about the things that divide us and look deeply for the common fears and aspirations that unite us. We have to enter these relationships understanding that this is more than mere cultural exchange. This is Christian community, in which we are expected to speak the truth in love, confess and repent, and offer forgiveness.

I know this can be done and that it can be fruitful because I've been doing it for the eighteen months or so that I've been writing this book. My wife (the city girl) and I (the country boy) do not see eye to eye on everything we've covered in these pages. That has probably been true for the entirety of our marriage, but it has been absolutely clear for the last couple of years. As we've shared memories and debated issues, we have talked honestly and vulnerably. We have both been willing to admit that we likely are both wrong about some things and right about others. The conversations have been frustrating at times and awkward at times. But they have borne fruit. If you are married, you know that it would be very easy *not* to have the conversations. But we've chosen to have them. We've worked through some stuff. We're getting taller.

The circle is wider than that. If you count all my in-laws and such, I have family that lives across the country, in rural places, small towns, suburbia, and cities. They don't all know each other, but I know them all. And I know they would very likely *not* get along if they were all in the same room for a long period of time. (To be perfectly honest, I've sometimes daydreamed about arranging some sort of reunion that resulted in all of them in the same room and then sitting back to watch the sparks fly.)

I'm invested in this conversation because I love all of these people, even if they wouldn't like each other. My life today and every day is an amalgam of the lessons and values and skills and sensibilities they have, together, instilled in me through their love and care, in places as different as small-town Arkansas and the Chicago suburbs, rural Louisiana and Manhattan. I'm invested in this conversation because, ultimately, I believe that if Christ's church in America wants to bear witness to the kingdom of God on earth, we have to figure out how to rally around our identity as His children and render all other identities secondary. I'm invested because our testimony as ministers of reconciliation is only as strong as our commitment to be a reconciled body, here and now.

And I'm *hopeful* because God, in Christ, has given us everything we need to move toward each other in faith.

Acknowledgments

It would be impossible to identify everyone whose input or conversation or friendship improved this book. Many of them are identified in the stories you've just read. Two deserve special acknowledgment.

One of them is my coworker Robert Elkin. He and I hashed out a lot of this material informally during lunchtime conversations over the last year. Those conversations made this book better.

The other is my wife, Amy. Without her profound insights, I would still be trying to figure out what many of these stories mean. She has helped me understand our shared experiences as well as my childhood experiences in deeper and redeeming ways. The truth is, she deserves a coauthor credit for everything I write, as she is the iron that sharpens all of my thinking.

Notes

This Is How It Is with Us: An Introduction

1. The amount of material on this subject can be overwhelming. I recommend the following as helpful introductions: Dante Chinni and James Gimpel, *Our Patchwork Nation: The Surprising Truth About the "Real" America: The 12 Community Types that Make Up America* (New York: Gotham Books, 2010); Charles Murray, *Coming Apart: The State of White America, 1960-2010* (New York: Crown Forum, 2012); Elizabeth Currid-Halkett, *The Sum of Small Things: A Theory of the Aspirational Class* (Princeton: Princeton University Press, 2017).

2. Michael O. Emerson and Christian Smith, *Divided by Faith: Evangelical Religion and the Problem of Race in America* (New York: Oxford University Press, 2001), remains an excellent overview of this issue, especially as it relates to people of faith in America. See also Richard Rothstein, *The Color of Law: A Forgotten History of How Our Government Segregated America* (New York: Liveright, 2017), for a compelling introduction to the idea of systemic injustice as it applies to real estate.

3. "Political Polarization in the American Public: How Increasing Ideological Uniformity and Partisan Antipathy Affect Politics, Compromise and Everyday Life," Pew Research Center, June 12, 2014, https://www.people-press.org/2014/06/12/political-polarization-in-the-american-public/.

4. For example, Emily Guskin, "Americans Are Scattered and Divided Over Which Source They Most Trust for News," *The Washington Post*, December 19, 2018, https://www.washingtonpost.com/politics/2018/12/19/americans-are-scattered-divided-over-which-source-they-most-trust-news/.

5. Lindsay MacDonald, "These Are the Most Popular Shows on Netflix by State," TVGuide.com, December 20, 2018, https://www.tvguide.com/news/most-popular-netflix-show-by-state/.

6. Emily Badger, "Rural and Urban Americans, Equally Convinced the Rest of the Country Dislikes Them," The Upshot, *The New York Times*, May 22, 2018, https://www.nytimes.com/2018/05/22/upshot/rural-and-urban-residents-feel-disparaged-pew-survey.html.

7. Kim Parker, Juliana Menasce Horowitz, Anna Brown, Richard Fry, D'Vera Cohn, and Ruth Igielnik, "What Unites and Divides Urban, Suburban and Rural Communities," Pew Research Center, May 22, 2018, http://www.pewsocialtrends.org/2018/05/22/what-unites-and-divides-urban-suburban-and-rural-communities.

8. For example, Michael Lipka and Gregory A. Smith, "Like Americans Overall, U. S. Catholics Are Sharply Divided by Party," Pew Research Center, January 24, 2019, https://www.pewresearch .org/fact-tank/2019/01/24/like-americans-overall-u-s-catholics-are-sharply-divided-by-party/.

9. Glenn Daman, *The Forgotten Church: Why Rural Ministry Matters for Every Church in America* (Chicago: Moody, 2018), 16.

10. Ashley Hales, *Finding Holy in the Suburbs: Living Faithfully in the Land of Too Much* (Downers Grove, IL: IVP Books, 2018), 8.

11. *The Strategically Small Church: Intimate, Nimble, Authentic and Effective* (Minneapolis: Bethany House Publishers, 2010); *Misreading Scripture with Western Eyes: Removing Cultural Blinders to Better Understand the Bible* (Downers Grove, IL: IVP Books, 2012); *Paul Behaving Badly: Was the Apostle a Racist, Chauvinist Jerk?* (Downers Grove: IVP Books, 2016); *Demanding Liberty: An Untold Story of American Religious Liberty* (Downers Grove, IL: IVP Books, 2018).

Chapter 1: A Nice Place to Belong To

1. G. K. Chesterton, *Orthodoxy* (San Francisco: Ignatius Press, 1995), 72. Originally published in 1908.

2. Ibid.

3. Matt Carmichael, "How Many States Has the Average American Visited?," Livability, July 25, 2016, https://livability.com/topics/ business/how-many-states-has-the-average-american-visited.

4. Quoctrung Bui and Claire Cain Miller, "The Typical American Lives Only 18 Miles from Mom," The Upshot, *The New York Times*, December 23, 2015, https://www.nytimes.com/interactive/2015/12/24/ upshot/24up-family.html.

Chapter 2: What We Mean When We Talk About "Urban" and "Rural" America

1. Shannan Martin, *The Ministry of Ordinary Places: Waking Up to God's Goodness Around You* (Nashville: Nelson Books, 2018), xvii. The author now lives in Goshen, Indiana, which had a population of 33,220 in 2017.

2. "The Federal Definition of 'Rural'—Times 15," Politics, *The Washington Post*, https://www.washingtonpost.com/politics/the-federal-definition-of-rural--times-15/2013/06/08/a39e46a8-cd4a-11e2-ac03-178510c9cc0a_story.html.

3. Nate Berg, "U.S. Urban Population Is Up . . . But What Does 'Urban' Really Mean?," CityLab, March 26, 2012, https://www.citylab.com/ equity/2012/03/us-urban-population-what-does-urban-really-mean/ 1589.

4. Jed Kolko, "How Suburban Are Big American Cities?," FiveThirtyEight, May 21, 2015, https://fivethirtyeight.com/features/how-suburban-are-big-american-cities.

5. Parker, Horowitz, Brown, Fry, Cohn, and Igielnik, "What Unites and Divides Urban, Suburban and Rural Communities."

6. Tara Bahrampour, "Cities Growing More Slowly than Suburbs for the First Time in Six Years," *The Washington Post*, May 25, 2017, https://www.washingtonpost.com/local/social-issues/cities-growing-more-slowly-than-suburbs-for-the-first-time-in-six-years/2017/05/24/aeee0f36-40bc-11e7-adba-394ee67a7582_story.html?utm_term=.56c562b97fe6.

7. Danielle Kurtzleben, "What We Mean When We Talk About 'Suburban Women Voters," Politics: NPR, April 7, 2018, https://www.npr.org/2018/04/07/599573817/what-we-mean-when-we-talk-about-suburban-women-voters.

8. Robert Groves, "Rural and Suburban America: When One Definition is not Enough," United States Census Bureau, August 2, 2011, www.census.gov/newsroom/blogs/director/2011/08/rural-and-suburban-america-when-one-definition-is-not-enough.html.

Chapter 3: Three Degrees of Separation

1. Robert Wuthnow, *The Left Behind: Decline and Rage in Rural America* (Princeton: Princeton University Press, 2018), 4.

2. Harry Black, "Talk Number Two: Immodestly Dressed Young People," in *Fifteen Plain Talks to Young People* (Los Angeles: n.d.), 5.

3. Jacob Shelton, "Inside Extreme Evangelical Hell Houses," Graveyard Shift, https://www.ranker.com/list/inside-evangelical-hell-houses/jacob-shelton?utm_source=facebook&utm_medium=creepy&pgid=1011190218967434&utm_campaign=inside-evangelical-hell-houses; Josiah Hesse, "Evangelical Hell Houses Are Waking Nightmares," October 30, 2017, https://www.vice.com/en_us/article/3kvkmy/evangelical-hell-houses-are-waking-nightmares; Scaremare, Liberty University, https://www.liberty.edu/scaremare/.

4. Chinni and Gimpel, *Our Patchwork Nation*, 54.

Chapter 4: Making Life Imaginable

1. Robert Wuthnow, *Remaking the Heartland: Middle America since the 1950s* (Princeton: Princeton UP, 2011), 82.

2. "Bentonville, Arkansas Population," CensusViewer, http://censusviewer.com/city/AR/Bentonville.

3. The trend as of 2010 (see http://www.arkansasonline.com/census/).

4. "Minden, Louisiana Population," CensusViewer, http://censusviewer. com/city/LA/Minden.

5. "Zachary, Louisiana Population," CensusViewer, http://censusviewer. com/city/LA/Zachary.

6. Wendell Berry, *What Are People For?*, 2nd ed. (Berkeley, CA: Counterpoint, 2010), 158.

7. Ibid., 71.

8. Ibid., 71–72.

Chapter 5: The Kind of Place You Leave

1. Bruce Springsteen, "Born to Run," Born to Run (album), August 25, 1975, Columbia.

2. Henry David Thoreau, *Walden* (New York: Thomas Y. Crowell & Company, 1910), 118.

3. George M. Weston, *The Poor Whites of the South* (Washingon, DC: Buell & Blanchard, 1856), 5.

4. Nancy Isenberg, *White Trash: The 400-Year Untold History of Class in America* (New York: Penguin, 2016), 107.

5. Edward Alsworth Ross, *Foundations of Sociology* (London: Macmillan Company, 1910), 302–304, emphasis added.

6. Henry Louis Mencken, *H. L. Mencken on Religion* (Amherst, NY: Prometheus, 2002), 172.

7. "Urban and Rural Areas," United States Census Bureau, https:// www.census.gov/history/www/programs/geography/urban_and_ rural_areas.html.

8. Bruce Springsteen, "Thunder Road," Born to Run (album), August 25, 1975, Columbia.

9. Bruce Springsteen, "Born to Run," Born to Run (album), August 25, 1975, Columbia.

Chapter 6: You Never Know What Might Happen to You in the Suburbs

1. Ian Stansel, "The Fictional Suburbs," *PloughShares*, Emerson College, March 7, 2013, http://blog.pshares.org/index.php/ the-fictional-suburbs.

2. J. D. Vance, *Hillbilly Elegy* (New York: HarperCollins, 2016), 202.

3. Philip Jenkins, *The Next Christendom: The Coming of Global Christianity* (New York: Oxford University Press, 2002).

4. Philip Jenkins, *The New Faces of Christianity: Believing the Bible in the Global South* (New York: Oxford University Press, 2006).

5. Kathleen Norris, "Dakota: Or, Gambling, Garbage, and the New Ghost Dance," in *Dakota: A Spiritual Geography* (Boston: Houghton Mifflin, 2001), 32.

Chapter 7: Learning to Tell the Whole Truth

1. Chimamanda Ngozi Adichie, "The Danger of a Single Story," TEDGlobal 2009 transcript, https://www.ted.com/talks/chimamanda _adichie_the_danger_of_a_single_story/transcript.
2. Ibid., 4:37.
3. Ibid., 5:44.
4. Ibid., 8:42.
5. Ibid., 12:45.
6. Ed Pilkington, "Obama angers midwest voters with guns and religion remark: Comments seized on by Hillary Clinton, who hopes to turn voters against what she classes as Obama's revealed 'elitism'," *The Guardian*, April 14, 2008, https://www.theguardian.com/world/2008/ apr/14/barackobama.uselections2008.
7. Adichie, "The Danger of a Single Story."
8. I talk about my experience in such a church in some detail in *The Strategically Small Church*.
9. Wendell Berry, "God and Country," in *What Are People For?*, 2nd ed. (Berkeley, CA: Counterpoint, 2010), 97.

Chapter 8: A New York State of Mind

1. David Sedaris, *Me Talk Pretty One Day* (Boston: Little, Brown and Company, 2000), 126.
2. Walker Percy, *The Moviegoer* (New York: Alfred A. Knopf, 1961), 98.
3. "Total Parkland as Percent of City Land Area," FY 2009, The Trust for Public Land, http://cloud.tpl.org/pubs/ccpe_Acreage_and_ Employees_Data_2010.pdf.
4. Kim Brooks, "Motherhood in the Age of Fear," *New York Times*, July 27, 2018, https://www.nytimes.com/2018/07/27/opinion/sunday/ motherhood-in-the-age-of-fear.html?smid=fb-nytimes&smtyp=cur.
5. Jody Mercier, "Adventure Playground on Gov. Island Debuts 2018 Schedule and Name," Mommy Poppins, April 6, 2018, www .mommypoppins.com/new-york-city-kids/parks-playgrounds/ the-adventure-playground-on-governors-island-gets-a-new-name.
6. E. B. White, "Transient," in *The Second Tree from the Corner* (New York: Harper & Row, 1954), 220–21.
7. F. Scott Fitzgerald, *This Side of Paradise* (New York: Oxford University Press, 2009), 217.
8. White, "In an Elevator," in *The Second Tree from the Corner*, 227.
9. Summarized from Robert W. Snyder, *Crossing Broadway: Washington Heights and the Promise of New York City* (New York: Three Hills, 2014).

Chapter 9: Common Cause in the Kingdom

1. Glenn Daman, *The Forgotten Church: Why Rural Ministry Matters for Every Church in America* (Chicago: Moody Publishers, 2018), 143.
2. Drew Hyun, "5 Common Mistakes of Urban Church Planters," NewChurches.com, March 28, 2017, https://newchurches.com/blogs/5-common-mistakes-urban-church-planters.
3. Daman, *The Forgotten Church*, 143.
4. J. Allen Thompson, "Unique Challenges Facing Urban Church Planters," Gospel in Life, May 20, 2009, https://gospelinlife.com/downloads/unique-challenges-facing-urban-church-planters/.
5. "2012 Profile of All North American Megachurches," Hartford Institute for Religion Research, www.hirr.hartsem.edu/megachurch/megastoday_profile.html.
6. Barney Warf and Morton Winsberg, "Geographies of Megachurches in the United States," *Journal of Cultural Geography* 27, no. 1 (February 2010): 41.

Chapter 10: The Flip Side

1. Steve Katz, *Florry of Washington Heights* (London: Serpent's Tail, 1988), 7.
2. Abigail Hauslohner and Emily Guskin, "Differences, in black and white: Rural Americans' views often set apart by race," *The Washington Post*, June 19, 2017, https://www.washingtonpost.com/national/differences-in-black-and-white-rural-americans-views-often-set-apart-by-race/2017/06/16/9e3b8164-47c9-11e7-a196-a1bb629f64cb_story.html?noredirect=on&utm_term=.fd65178e3ba6.
3. See Raz Robinson, "Black Parents Are Avoiding America's White Suburbs to Keep Their Kids Safe," Fatherly, September 12, 2018, https://www.fatherly.com/love-money/culture/black-parents-race-suburbs-childrens-safety/; Gregory Smithsimon, "Are African American Families More Vulnerable in a Largely White Neighborhood?," The Guardian, February 21, 2018, https://www.theguardian.com/books/2018/feb/21/racial-segregation-in-america-causes; Sandra E. Garcia, "Black Boys Feel Less Safe in White Neighborhoods, Study Shows," New York Times, August 14, 2018, https://www.nytimes.com/2018/08/14/us/black-boys-white-neighborhoods-fear.html.
4. Katz, *Florry of Washington Heights*, 7.
5. Niraj Chokshi, "Diversity in America's Counties, in 5 Maps," *Washington Post*, June 30, 2014, https://www.washingtonpost.com/blogs/govbeat/wp/2014/06/30/diversity-in-americas-counties-in-5-maps/.

6. Tim Keller, "All of Life is Repentance," Cru, www.cru.org/us/en/train-and-grow/spiritual-growth/all-of-life-is-repentance.html.

Chapter 11: Check Your Mirrors

1. Jennifer Grant, *Maybe God Is Like That Too* (Minneapolis: Sparkhouse Family, 2017).
2. "Prayerfully Reviewing Your Day: The Daily Examen," Loyola Press, https://www.loyolapress.com/our-catholic-faith/prayer/personal-prayer-life/different-ways-to-pray/prayerfully-reviewing-your-day-daily-examen.

Chapter 12: Pray Like It's Your Sacred Place

1. Eugene H. Peterson, *A Long Obedience in the Same Direction: Discipleship in an Instant Society*, 2nd ed. (Downers Grove: IVP Books, 2000), 51–52.
2. Timothy Keller, *The Prodigal Prophet: Jonah and the Mystery of God's Mercy* (New York: Viking, 2018), 12.
3. Ibid.
4. "Evangelical and Non-evangelical Voting & Views of Politics in America--Part 1," LifeWay Research, Lifewayresearch.com/wp-content/uploads/2018/10/Voting-and-Views-of-Politics-in-America-Part-1.pdf.

IS THE CHURCH BECOMING POLARIZED TOO?

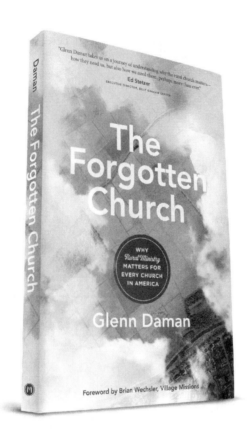

The Forgotten Church addresses the divide between rural and suburban/urban churches. It describes rural ministry today, explores opportunities recent trends provide, and showcases the remarkable benefits of suburban, urban, and rural churches working together. This book is essential for any pastor, because we are one body, and we need each other.

978-0-8024-1813-5 | also available as an eBook

BIBLICAL MISSIONS
FOR ANY BLOCK

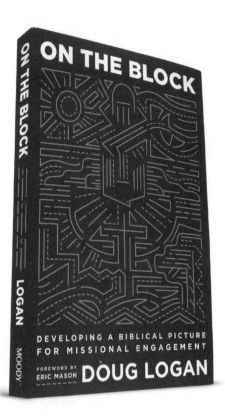

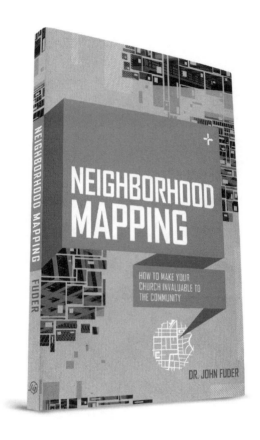